PYTHON:
THE NO-NONSENSE GUIDE

Learn Python Programming Within 12 Hours!

Cyberpunk University

Disclaimer Notice:

Table of Contents

Introduction 1

Hour 1: Getting Started with Python 2

1.1 What is Python? 2

1.2 Top Benefits of Learning Python Programming 3

1.3 Who is this book meant for? 3

1.4 Installing Python and Text Editor 4

1.4.1 Alternative Text Editors 6

1.5 Hello World! Your First Program 7

1.6 Running saved .py files 9

Hour 2: Variables, Strings and Basic Data Types 12

2.1 Variables 12

2.1.1 How to assign values to variables 12

2.1.2 Multiple variable assignments 14

2.2 Standard Data Types 14

2.2.1 Numbers 15

2.2.2 Strings 15

2.2.3 Lists 16

2.2.4 Tuples 18

2.2.5 Dictionaries 19

2.2.6 Comments 20

Hour 3: User Input, Basic Math, and Output 21

3.1 input () 21

3.2 More Numbers 22

3.2.1 Number Type Conversion 23

3.2.2 Basic Math Operators 24
3.2.3 Comparison Operators 26
3.2.4 Order of Operations 28
3.3 Output: Printing to the screen 29
Hour 4: If-Statements 31
4.1 Decision making 32
4.2 Single IF Statement 33
4.3 If… Else 33
4.4 Elif 34
4.5 Nested IF Statements 36
Hour 5: Loops 38
5.1 The while loop 39
5.1.1 Else Statement with While 41
5.2 The for loop 42
5.2.1 Else Statement with For Loop 44
5.4 Loop Control Statements 45
5.4.1 Pass statement 45
5.4.2 Break statement 46
5.4.3 Continue statement 48
5.5 Indentation 49
Hour 6: Functions 51
6.1 Defining a Function 51
6.2 Calling a Function 54
6.3 Time-saving functions 55

6.4 Pass by reference vs. value 55
6.5 Function Arguments 58
6.5.1 Required arguments 58
6.5.2 Keyword arguments 59
6.5.3 Default arguments 61
6.5.4 Variable-length arguments 62
6.6 The return Statement 62
Hour 7: Dictionaries 64
7.1 Keys and Values of the Dictionary 64
7.2 Accessing Values in Dictionary 65
7.3 Updating the Dictionary 67
7.3.1 Modifying Dictionary Elements 67
7.3.2 Deleting Dictionary Elements 68
7.4 Properties of Dictionary Keys 69
7.5 Built-in Dictionary Functions and Methods 69
Hour 8: Classes 72
8.1 Overview of Terminologies used in OOP 72
8.2 Creating Classes 73
8.3 Creating Instance Objects 75
8.4 Accessing and Working with Attributes 77
8.5 Built-In Class Attributes 80
8.6 Class Inheritance 82
8.7 Overriding Methods 83
8.8 Overloading Operators 83
Hour 9: Files and Exceptions 85

9.1 Reading and Writing Files 85

9.1.1 The read() Method 86

9.1.2 The write() Method 89

9.2 File Positions 90

9.3 Renaming and Deleting Files 91

9.3.1 Renaming files using the rename() method 91

9.3.2 Deleting files using the remove() method 92

9.4 File and Directory Related Methods 93

Hour 10: Errors and Exceptions 94

10.1 Exception Handling 94

10.1.1 Table of Standard Exceptions 95

10.1.2 Exception Handling Syntax 96

10.2 Assertions 101

10.2.1 The asset statement 101

Hour 11: Testing Your Code 104

11.1 General rules of testing Python code 104

11.2 unittest 105

11.3 Doctest 106

11.4 Tools 107

11.4.1 py.test 107

11.4.2 Nose 107

11.4.3 tox 108

11.4.4 Unittest2 108

11.4.5 mock 108

Hour 12: Conclusion & Further Reading 109

Links 112

Tools 112

Course 113

Websites and Tutorials 113

Interactive Tools and Lessons 115

Introduction

You have made the right first stride towards becoming a hobbyist or a professional programmer using Python, one of the most widely used programming language on computers today. First off, welcome to a presentation of Cyberpunk University. Thank you for investing in this eBook, and we hope you will follow through it to learn how to develop your coding skills and become a Python programmer with ease within just days.

This eBook is structured into 12 practical chapters that take roughly an hour to do. We have designed the content of the book to be easy to follow for both complete beginners to programming and those with knowledge of other programming languages or have been introduced to Python partially before. The over 50 exercises distributed over the 12 hours of the course duration are an excellent way to get started learning to master all the essentials about Python.

Cyberpunk University is committed to producing content that helps learners discover their coding skills and to learn processes that make it easy for them to think of solutions to daily human problems. Many other programming books are coming in the future so be sure to check our catalog and get the chance to learn even more ways to write programs in different languages that computers can understand.

To help you get the most out of this book we have created the FREE "Cyberpunk Python Whizz Kit". The Kit contains an awesome cheat sheet to help you program as fast as possible and we've also included ALL the exercises from this book in python files. You can use them however you want.

DOWNLOAD THE FREE WHIZZ KIT HERE:

http://subscribe.cyberpunkuniversity.com

Hour 1: Getting Started with Python

Whether this is your initial foray into the world of programming, or you are learning Python to expand your programming skills set with a new language, you have come to the right place.

Every programmer has a story about they got into programming and what the first program they wrote was. This book is intended for complete beginners in the world of programming and Python in particular. We hope it will be useful enough for you to remember it when you tell the story of your path to being a successful professional or hobbyist programmer in the future.

This book focuses more on the practical aspects of writing code in Python. You do not need external resources to master the basics of Python programming, although some people find extensive researching even more useful. If you are a beginner in programming, I would recommend that you follow this guide exactly as instructed and only venture to wider research and practice after you understand the concepts each exercise it teaches. This will help prevent the confusion that arises from taking instructions from different sources.

This book is structured to guide you learn the essential basics of Python programming in 12 hours, each chapter representing an hour of code.

1.1 What is Python?

Everyone today knows what a computer is and understand why programmers are responsible for computers (including machines, Smartphone, cars, planes, etc.) doing what we 'command' them to. By learning to program computers, you have chosen to join the millions of programmers who strive to make life easier by writing programs in a computer language that instruct machines what to do. Python is one of these programs.

We can define Python as a very popular high-level, general-purpose, interpreted, and dynamic programming language that is very easy to learn. The design philosophy of Python focuses on code readability, and its syntax makes it easy for programmers to express the concepts in a computer program in fewer lines of code compared to other popular languages such as Java and C++.

1.2 Top Benefits of Learning Python Programming

Python is a general-purpose programming language. This means when you become a Python programmer, you can build just about anything from website back-end and artificial intelligence systems to desktop apps and robotic programs.

Because of its code readability, Python is a very easy to understand language and can be a perfect Launch pad for individuals hoping to go ahead and learn other more advanced languages. The language is governed by flexible rules, it offers limitless career opportunities to those who master it as a skill, and to put it simply, Python is the programming language of the future.

There is also a very vibrant and active support community with ready answers to all questions and concerns you may have during and after learning the basics. StackOverflow and Github are the best examples. The Python community is always willing to share meaning that most tools and libraries you will need to make your work easy will be just a simple search away.

1.3 Who is this book meant for?

To make use of this book, you must meet a few requirements:

1. Python is a cross-platform language. You must have a computer running Windows, Mac, or Linux operating system.

2. You must pay attention to detail. What typically separates good programs from bad ones is how meticulous they are in recognizing every element in the code, from a comma to space, and making sure every character is in its place.
3. You must have basic computer skills. This means you should be able to download and install a program, type, manipulate files on your computer, and know how to read and write (duh!).

1.4 Installing Python and Text Editor

Installing Python is simple. The most recent version of Python (Python 3.5 at the time of publication of this guide) is often included in many UNIX and Linux distributions.

Step 1: On your browser, go to www.python.org. Hover your pointer over the Download button and click Python 3.5.2 to download for your operating system. You will also need to know whether your operating system is 32-bit or 64-bit to download the correct version.

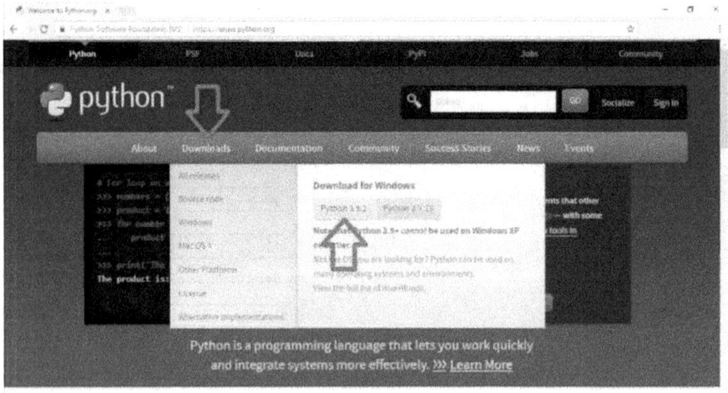

Fig 1.1 Downloading Python

If you need assistance at this point there is an invaluable resource for beginners here: https://wiki.python.org/moin/BeginnersGuide

You will also notice there are two versions of Python available for download: an older version 2.7.12 and the newer version 3.5. You can download and use either but in this book, we will be using Python 3.5.2. The beginner's guide above explains the difference between the two.

Step 2: Wait for the download to complete then run the installation.

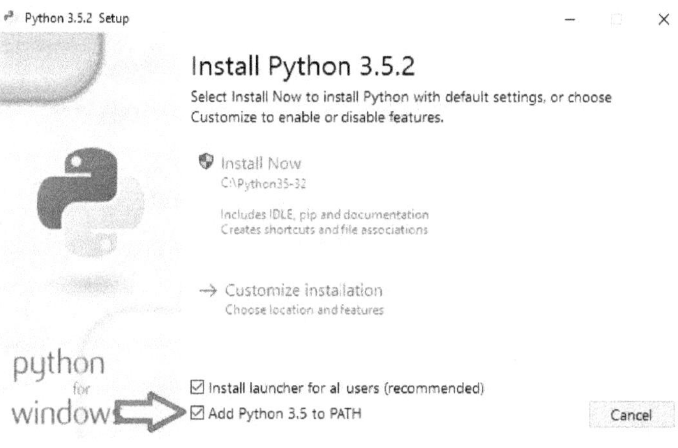

Fig 1.2: Installing Python

By default, Python installs to a directory on root with a name with version number embedded. For instance, if you are using Windows, your program should install in C:\Python35-32\. You can change install location by clicking 'Customize installation'.

Step 3: Check the **'Add Python 3.5 to PATH'** option and complete the installation. Leave all other options as they are.

Once an installation is complete, you will be able to write Python code as instructed in this book and run the code using an interactive interpreter that it is bundled with your installation. With the interpreter, you will be able to type commands line by line and see it run when you press enter.

You can start the Python Shell by clicking on the Python IDLE shortcut. It should be placed on the desktop, dock or start menu. You should see something like this:

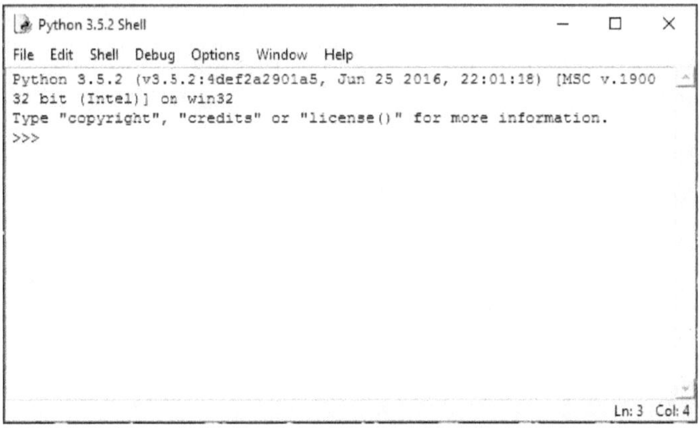

```
Python 3.5.2 Shell
File  Edit  Shell  Debug  Options  Window  Help
Python 3.5.2 (v3.5.2:4def2a2901a5, Jun 25 2016, 22:01:18) [MSC v.1900
32 bit (Intel)] on win32
Type "copyright", "credits" or "license()" for more information.
>>>
                                                        Ln: 3  Col: 4
```

Fig 1.3 Python Shell

Step 4: Create a folder inside the Python installation location to save your Python programs and name it 'Exfiles.' If you followed the instructions during setup and installed Python in C:\Python35-32\, then your practice files will be saved in C:\Python35-32\Exfiles\. It is very important you note the path of this folder because we will be using it a lot in executing scripts in the course of the book

1.4.1 Alternative Text Editors

A good text editor is a must-have accessory if you look forward to being a good developer. Most text editors available on the internet have all the necessary tools you need to create and manage code, write down notes or just enjoy a distraction-free coding. You cannot use word processors such as MS

Word to write your code. The top 5 text editors with a free version that you can download and try are:

- Sublime Text (My favorite)
- Notepad++
- Vim (and its variations)
- Atom
- Text Wrangler (for Mac).

Personally, I prefer Sublime Text. For this course, you can use Notepad++ if you want a simple but powerful editor that you can get used to.

1.5 Hello World! Your First Program

To write your first program:

1. Start Python Shell or switch to the Python IDLE you started in step 3 above.
2. Type the following exactly as it appears, including, and especially, the text case:

print ("Hello World!")

```
Python 3.5.2 Shell
File Edit Shell Debug Options Window Help
Python 3.5.2 (v3.5.2:4def2a2901a5, Jun 25 2016, 22:01:18)
[MSC v.1900 32 bit (Intel)] on win32
Type "copyright", "credits" or "license()" for more infor
mation.
>>> print ("Hello World!")
Hello World!
>>> |
Ln: 5 Col: 4
```

Fig 1.4 Hello World!

Press Enter.

This is what you should see:

```
Python 3.5.2 Shell
File Edit Shell Debug Options Window Help
Python 3.5.2 (v3.5.2:4def2a2901a5, Jun 25 2016, 22:01:18)
[MSC v.1900 32 bit (Intel)] on win32
Type "copyright", "credits" or "license()" for more infor
mation.
>>> print ("Hello World!")
Hello World!
>>> |
Ln: 5 Col: 4
```

Fig 1.5 Hello World!

Save the file as HelloWorld.py in the 'ExFiles' directory you created during setup. Save the file by clicking 'File' then 'Save As.' Remember to enter the filename including the '.py.' extension each time. In this case, name your file "helloworld.py" then click 'Save.'

Congratulations! You are now a Python Programmer!

1.6 Running saved .py files

As I mentioned in Exercise 1, Python scripts are stored with an extension .py. Throughout this book, you will follow coding instructions and save files in a text editor before you can run them, unlike in exercise 1 where we used IDLE. In this section, I will show you how to run the Hello World! program you saved to show you what to do in every other exercise in this book.

To run the python scripts you will create during this course, and you will need to learn a few things about the command line. The instructions are pretty much the same for all platforms – Windows Power Shell and Linux and Mac Terminals.

Step 1: Start the command terminal (Powershell/Terminal) and type Python. On Mac, place a shortcut to your terminal on the dock for easier access.

In Windows, the Command Prompt should look like this:

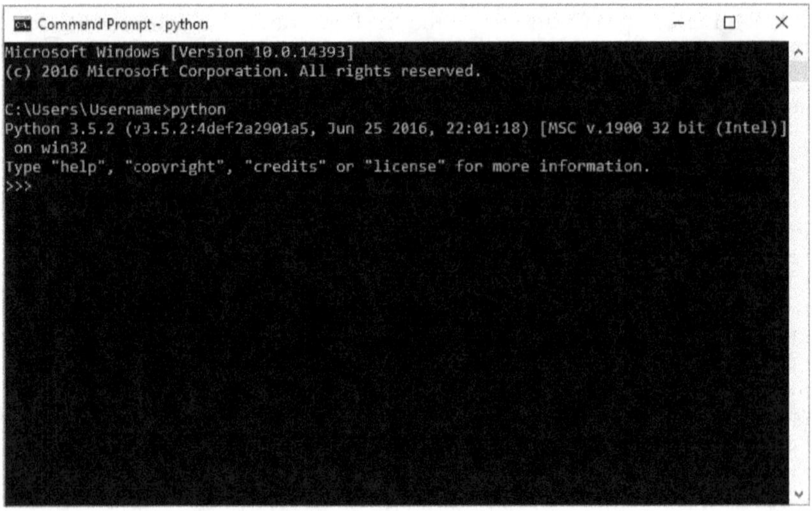

```
Command Prompt - python
Microsoft Windows [Version 10.0.14393]
(c) 2016 Microsoft Corporation. All rights reserved.

C:\Users\Username>python
Python 3.5.2 (v3.5.2:4def2a2901a5, Jun 25 2016, 22:01:18) [MSC v.1900 32 bit (Intel)]
 on win32
Type "help", "copyright", "credits" or "license" for more information.
>>>
```

Fig 1.6: Windows Command Prompt

Step 2: You can run Python by typing the word Python on your command line. Try it.

To quit python and return to the terminal program, press Ctrl+Z (^Z) or type the command **exit().**

Step 3: To run a Python script you saved in ExFiles folder, you will learn to go to the directory on the command line. First, quit python by pressing Ctrl+Z or using the **exit()** command then type "cd.." and press to move a level up and again till you are on the root of your drive.

Step 4: Change directory to ExFiles by typing "cd C:\Python35-32\ExFiles\"

Step 5: To run the helloworld.py script you saved in ExFiles, while on the terminal, type:

Python helloworld.py

You will be using this process to execute the Python exercise scripts you will write while we progress with this course. Do not worry if it looks complicated, you will get used to these steps.

Hour 2: Variables, Strings and Basic Data Types

This hour, we will learn the basics of what makes up a program script.

2.1 Variables

Variables are reserved memory spaces that store values. Simply put, when you create a variable, you reserve some memory space to store certain data when the program is executed.

The Python interpreter determines the memory be allocated and the data to be stored in it depending on the values you assign the variables. By assigning different data types to the variables, the interpreter reserves spaces for integers, numbers with decimals, or text characters.

2.1.1 How to assign values to variables

Variables are automatically declared when you assign a value to a variable using the equal sign (=) such that variable = value. For instance, in my_age=22, the variable called "my_age" has a value of 22.

Ex1

Start your editor and enter the following Python code. Be careful not to miss the commas or misspell the variable names.

```
#Ex1

product_ID = 10                 #Integer variable assignment

product_price = 2.5             #float variable assignment
```

```
product_name = “Soda”        #String variable assignment



print (product_ID)

print (product_price)

print (product_name)
```

In this exercise, you assigned the variables product_ID, product_price, and product_name different values then commanded the interpreter to display those values using print. If you get an error, check and re-check your spelling and commas and ensure everything is EXACTLY as it appears. The result should look like this when you run Ex1.py script:

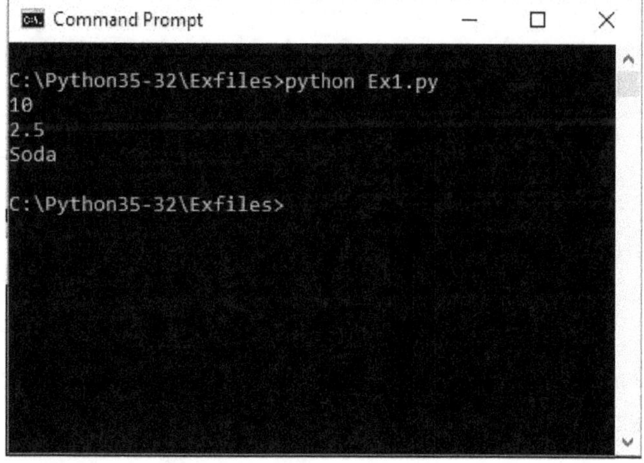

Do not worry about the types of assignments. We will discuss them later in the book.

2.1.2 Multiple variable assignments

When dealing with several related variables, you can assign one value to several variables simultaneously e.g.

```
x = y = z = 2
```

In this example, the integer value 2 is created and the variables x, y and z memory locations are assigned to the integer value. You can also assign multiple variables different values at a go. For example, in Ex1, we could have easily assigned the variables as follows:

```
product_ID, product_price, product_name = 10, 2.5, "Soda"
```

The variables product_ID, product_price, and product_name are assigned values 10, 2.5, and "Soda" respectively.

Edit the code in Ex1 to assign the variables values as shown above then save the .py file and run it on the terminal. Does the program behave the same?

2.2 Standard Data Types

Python has five standard types of data that define operations that can be carried out on them as well as how they are stored in memory. They five data types we will cover in this section are:

- Numbers
- Strings
- Lists
- Tuples
- Dictionary
- Comments

2.2.1 Numbers

Numbers are essentially numeric values that are created when a value is assigned to them. For instance, when you create a variable my_age and assign it a value of 22, the number 22 is created. There are three different types of numbers you will be working with:

Integers (int) – These are long integers e.g. 1, -12, 02.00, 372, 18374, -1862, -0x260, 100000,

Floats (float) – These are numbers with decimal points e.g. 1.0, 0.5, -734.2, 13.90201, 32.3+e18, -32.54e100, 0490

Complex – These are numbers with ordered pairs of real floating-point numbers written x + yj where j is an imaginary unit. How complex do 3.14j, 45.j, 9.322e-36j, 876j, -.6545+0J, 3e+26J, 4.53e-7j look?

In the next chapter, we will dive deeper into numbers and even use various operators to manipulate them.

2.2.2 Strings

Think of these as plain characters within single or double quotation marks. A string is created by enclosing text and numbers in either single or double quotes and can be declared with a star. You will get to use strings a lot.

Ex2

```
#Ex2

str1 = "Hello World!"



print (str1)                    #Displays the entire string contents
```

```
print (str1[0])              #Displays the first character in a string

print (str1[2:])             #Displays from the 3rd character in a string

print (str1*3)               #Displays the string content 3 times

print (str1[1:3])            #Displays characters 2 to 4 in a string

print ("Testing", str1)      #Displays a concatenated string.
```

Start Python Shell and enter the following string operations to see what they do:

Here is what you should see when you run the script.

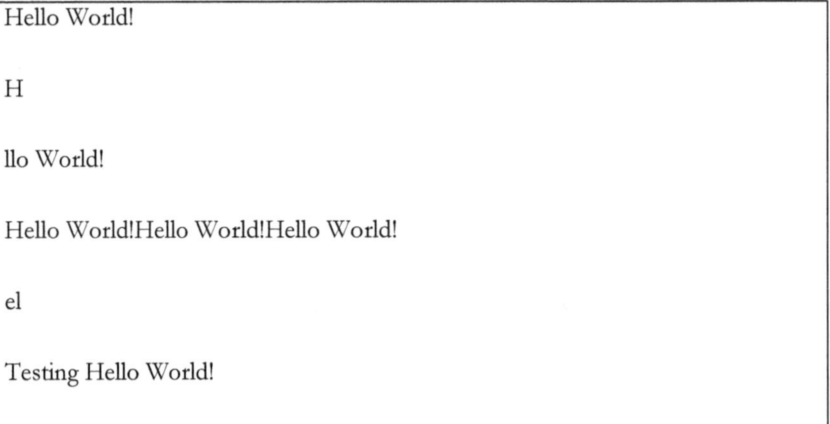

Hello World!

H

llo World!

Hello World!Hello World!Hello World!

el

Testing Hello World!

2.2.3 Lists

A list contains separate items enclosed within square brackets [ ] and are separated by commas. The values on a list can be accessed using the same slice operators [ ] and [:] just like with strings. Also, just as with strings, the + sign is the concatenation while the * is the repletion operation symbol.

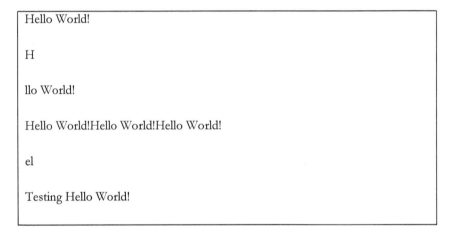

Ex3

Start your code editor and enter the following code as it appears:

```
#Ex3

fruits_list = ["oranges", "bananas", "peaches", "mangoes"]

vegs_list = ["kales", "cabbages"]



print (fruits_list)                #Displays the entire fruits_list list

print (fruits_list[0])             #Displays the first item in the list

print (fruits_list[2:4])           #Displays items 3 through 5 in the list

print (vegs_list * 3)              #Displays the list three times

print (fruits_list[1:])            #Displays item 2 onwards

print (fruits_list[:2])            #Displays all items to the third

print (vegs_list + fruits_list)    #Displays concatenated lists
```

When you run the script above, the result should look like this:

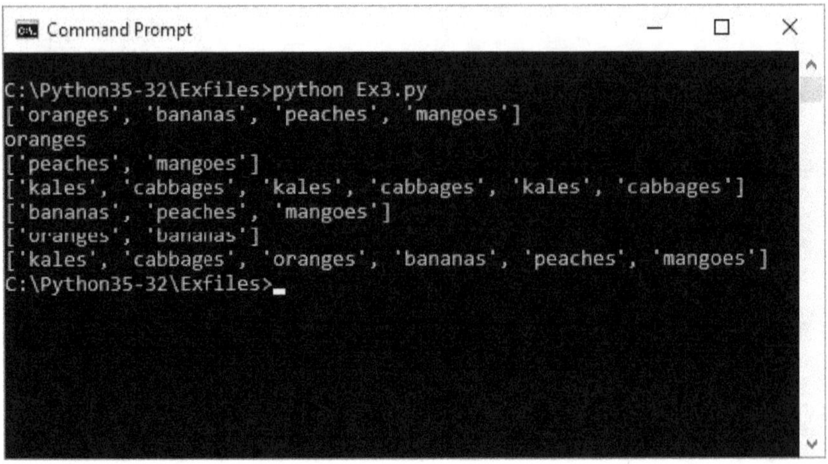

```
Command Prompt
C:\Python35-32\Exfiles>python Ex3.py
['oranges', 'bananas', 'peaches', 'mangoes']
oranges
['peaches', 'mangoes']
['kales', 'cabbages', 'kales', 'cabbages', 'kales', 'cabbages']
['bananas', 'peaches', 'mangoes']
['oranges', 'bananas']
['kales', 'cabbages', 'oranges', 'bananas', 'peaches', 'mangoes']
C:\Python35-32\Exfiles>_
```

2.2.4 Tuples

Tuples are a lot like lists in that they are a collection of sequential data. A tuple is made up of values separated by commas and enclosed in parentheses (). The main difference between lists and tuples (besides one using square brackets and the other parentheses) is that the items defined in a list can be changed (updated) while those in tuples cannot. Most operations on tuples are similar to those of lists.

Ex4

```
#Ex4

tup_1 = (‘London’, 2017, ‘$20.00’, 5.2, “x”)

tup_2 = (60,”magic”,2017,”5.0”)



print (tup_1[0], tup_2)

print (tup_2, tup1[1:3])
```

```
print (tup_2*2)
```

Like strings and lists, tuple indexes start at 0 and can be concatenated, sliced, and so on.

2.2.5 Dictionaries

In Python, a dictionary is a kind of hash table type that works like associative arrays with key-value pairs enclosed in curly braces { }. A dictionary can have almost any type of data but typically it contains numbers and strings. Values are often any arbitrary Python objects.

Ex5

Dictionaries

```
#Ex5

foods = {"fruit" : "apple", "vegetable" : "kale", "meat" : "beef", "carb" : "cereal"}



print (foods)

print (foods["vegetable"])
```

Dictionaries do not have any concept of order when it comes to elements and can be said to be “out of order” or simply “unordered”. In hour 7, we will look at dictionaries more exhaustively.

2.2.6 Comments

Comments are not particularly a data type, but every programming language needs them because they are essential to human developers. Comments, denoted with the hash character (#), are used to tell the human reader what a particular code means or does in plain language.

They are also used to disable parts of the program when you need to remove them temporarily. The best example of using comments is demonstrated in Ex3. Note that Python ignores everything in a line of code beginning with the #. In fact, your text editor should color comments differently to show you what the interpreter will ignore.

Hour 3: User Input, Basic Math, and Output

Every computer program is written to solve a problem, and as such, it must accept some form of input from the user. In most cases, the input is through the keyboard. For this purpose, Python provides the input() function to enter data. The prompt string is an optional input parameter you will learn about later.

3.1 input ()

When you use input(), the program flow will stop until the user enters the expected data and press enter when the input function is called. The input text will be displayed on the screen.

The input the user enters is returned as a string without modification. Other functions such as casting and eval that you will learn later are used to transform the data into a different depending on the purpose of the program and variables declared.

Ex6

Input

Write the following code:

```
#Ex6

name = input("What is your name: ")

age = input("How old are you?: ")

location = input("Where do you live?: ")
```

```
print ("You are ", name, "from", location, "and you are", age, "years old.")
```

Save the script in your practice files folder and run it. This is what you should see:

```
name = input("What is your name: ")

What is your name: John

age = input("How old are you?: ")

How old are you?: 22

location = input("Where do you live?: ")

Where do you live?: London



print ("You are ", name, "from", location, "and you are", age, "years old.")

You are John from London and you are 22 years old.
```

3.2 More Numbers

Considering that numbers are immutable data types, changing the value of an assigned number data type will result in a newly allocated object. This also means that when assign a value to a number object, a new one is created. For instance:

```
distance = 100
```

```
time = x = 6



x = int(input ("Time in seconds: "))

speed = distance / time
```

Example 3.2

In the above example, the value that the user enters will replace the value of x which is 6.

3.2.1 Number Type Conversion

Before you can begin working with the different types of numbers you are already familiar with, you must know how to convert from one type to another. The most typical conversion is converting strings to integers and floats and converting between floats and integers. These are what you need to know now.

In example 3.2, because the user input is a string by default, we used int() to convert it to an integer before we can use it to calculate speed. Python converts expressions with mixed data types internally. The expressions employed in the conversion are:

- To convert x to a plain integer type int(x)
- To convert x to a floating-point number type float(x)
- To convert x to a complex number with real part x type complex(x)

3.2.2 Basic Math Operators

Every programming language needs to have a way of calculating numbers and math to make it useful. This section deals a lot about symbols. You are probably already familiar with the operation symbols you will use to carry out comparisons and calculations because they are standard:

+ plus (add)

- minus (subtract)

/ slash (divide)

* asterisk (multiply)

< less than

> greater than

<= less than or equal

>= greater than or equal

% percent

Ex7

Let us use these symbols in this exercise. Code the following script

```
#Ex7

print ("Now I will count my fruits")



mangoes = 6 + 8 + 2
```

```
apples = 9 / 3 + 1

peaches = 4 * 3 - 2



print ("Mangoes", mangoes)

print ("Apples", apples)

print ("Peaches", peaches)



print ("How many fruits have I eaten?")

mangoes_left = int(input ("How many mangoes are left?"))

apples_left = int(input ("How many apples are left?"))

peaches_left = int(input ("How many peaches are left?"))



#Now let us calculate the number of fruits eaten

mangoes_eaten = mangoes - mangoes_left

apples_eaten = apples - apples_left

peaches_eaten = peaches - peaches_left



print ("You have eaten ", mangoes_eaten, "mangoes,", apples_eaten, "apples, and ", peaches_eaten, "peaches.")
```

In this exercise, first we use random numbers to calculate how many fruits we have then we display the result. The program then prompts for input (integers) of the number of fruits left which it uses to calculate how many we have eaten. Follow each line of code to understand what it does and where you could improve fully.

3.2.3 Comparison Operators

So far we have looked at and used mathematical operators. Python allows you to compare values on either side of an equation and decides how they relate. Here is a breakdown of these relational operators:

==	equal	The condition becomes true if the values of two operands are equal	(x == y)
!=	not equal	The condition becomes true if the values of two operands are not equal	(x != y)
>	Greater than	The condition becomes true if the value of the left operand is greater than that of the right	(x > y)
<	Less than	The condition becomes true if the value of the left operand is less than that of the right	(x < y)
>=	Greater than or equal	The condition becomes true if the value of the left operand is equal to or greater than of the right	(x >= y)
<=	Less than or equal	The condition becomes true if the value on the left operand is equal to or less than that of the right	(x <= y)

Ex8

```
#Ex8

#Program to determine whether a shape is a rectangle or a square and calculate its area and perimeter.
```

```
height = float(input("Enter the height of the shape: "))

length = float(input("Enter the width of the shape: "))



if (height == length):

        shape = "square"

else:

        shape = "rectangle"



area = (height * length)

perimeter = ((length + height)*2)



print ("The shape is a", shape, "with an area of ", area, "and perimeter of ",
perimeter)
```

Can you change the data types for height and length to integer and see what answers you get?

Precedence	Operation	Definition
Highest	()	Anything in parentheses is computed first.
	**	Exponentiation
	-x, +x	Negation
	*, /, %, //	Multiplication, division, modulo,
	+, -	Addition, subtraction
	<, >, <=, >=, !=, ==	relational operators

	not	Logical
	and	Logical
Lowest	or	Logical

3.2.4 Order of Operations

It is a good practice always to indicate the order of operations when writing expressions in Python using parentheses (). If you do not, Python applies the standard order of operations you know from Algebra and Geometry in high school. Mathematical operations are evaluated in this PEMDAS order:

Ex9

```
#Ex9

#Example 1

x = 87 / 3 * 2 - 7 + 6

#1. 87 / 3 = 29

#2. 29 * 2 = 58

#3. 58 + 6 = 64

#4. 64 - 7 = 57

print ("89/3*2-4+6=", x)

#Example 2

x = 9 + 5 / 3 * 3

#1. 9 / 3 = 3

#2. 3 * 3 = 9
```

```
#3. 9 + 5 = 14

print ("9+5/3*3=", x)

#Example 3

x = 12 % 2 + 8 / 2 * 3

#Explain how this operation is carried out and check your answer

print ("12%2+8/2*3=", x)

#Example 4

x = (8 - 12) - 10 * 4

#Explain how this operation is carried out and check your answer

print ("(8-12)-10*4=", x)

#Example 5

x = 21 / 3 % 4 * 2 ** 3

#Explain how this operation is carried out and check your answer

print ("21/3%4*2**3=", x)
```

3.3 Output: Printing to the screen

The most straightforward way to output information is by using the print() statement. It passes none to multiple expressions separated by commas or combined by a plus sign (+) to display. This statement converts expressions into a string and displays the result as a standard output like this:

Ex10

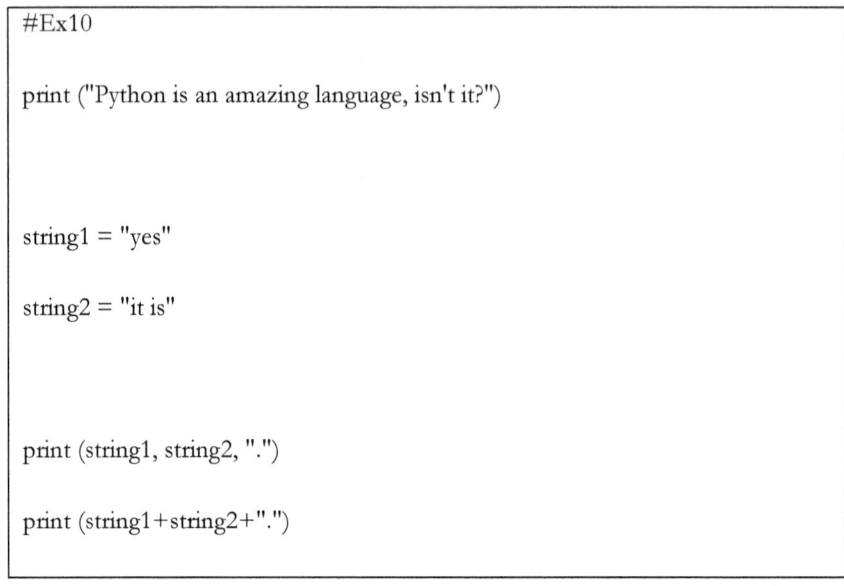

```
#Ex10

print ("Python is an amazing language, isn't it?")



string1 = "yes"

string2 = "it is"



print (string1, string2, ".")

print (string1+string2+".")
```

When you run this script, this is what will be displayed on your terminal screen:

```
C:\Python35-32\Exfiles>python Ex10.py

Python is an amazing language, isn't it?

yes it is .

yesit is.
```

Have you noticed any difference in how the output is spaced when you use comma or plus symbol to combine strings of text?

Hour 4: If-Statements

When you need a program you are writing to do something 20 times, you will not force the user to repeat instructions 20 times, you use iteration.

Iteration is when you write a code that tells the computer to repeat a task defined between two points until a certain condition is met.

Ex11

```
#Ex11

#This is a program to determine which fruits are more based on user input.

oranges = int(input("Enter the number of mangoes: "))

apples = int(input("Enter the number of apples: "))



if oranges < apples: #Checks if oranges are fewer than apples

        print ("There are more apples than oranges.")



if oranges > apples: #Checks if oranges are more than apples

        print ("There are more oranges than apples.")



if (oranges == apples): #Checks if the number of apples and oranges are equal

        print ("There are as many oranges as apples.")
```

4.1 Decision making

A computer program is essentially a set of instructions that guide it from the start to finish. Introducing an IF statement alters the linear start-to-finish plot of the program, allowing the program to make decisions and change the way it works. Here is a graphical representation of how the If statement affects how your code runs:

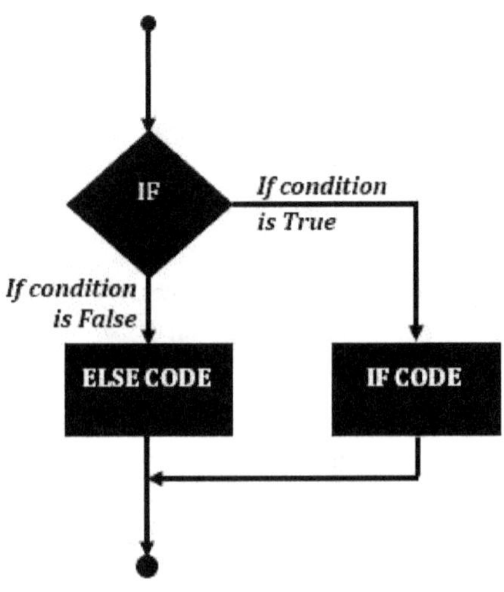

Fig 4: If decision flow chart

Ex12

Here is a simple exercise to determine whether a number a user enters is positive or negative.

```
#Ex12

num = int(input("Enter a positive or negative number: "))
```

```
if num > 0:

        print ("The number is a positive number!")

if num < 0:

        print ("The number is a negative number!")
```

This if statement includes a Boolean text condition expression. If the result of the test returns true, the print block of code is executed. If the test returns a false, the block is ignored.

4.2 Single IF Statement

If you write a block of code that consists of only one IF statement, it is acceptable to put the code condition in the same line as the header statement. For example:

```
num = 100

if (num == 100): print (“The value of num is 100!”)
```

4.3 If… Else

We can use If…Else when we need to have a block of code executed even when the Boolean test returns a negative. In Exercise 12, you will see how the block of code is executed as presented in fig 4.

Ex13

```
#Ex13

#A Program to determine the rate of discount based on price

price = int(input("Enter the price of the item: "))



if price < 100:

        discount = (price * 0.05)

        print ("The discount is ", discount)

else:

        discount = (price * 0.1)

        print ("The discount is ", discount)


print ("You will pay ", price - discount, "in total.")
```

In this exercise, the program asks the user to enter the price of an item then calculates the discount it qualifies for based on the price (5% for items worth less than 100 and 10% for the rest) then displays the discount and the final price of the item.

4.4 Elif

A step from the If...else statement is the Elif. As you may have guessed already, Elif is essentially a combination of Else and If in one statement. This statement allows the program to check multiple expressions and executes a block of code when one of the conditions returns TRUE. If all the conditions are FALSE, the block of code will be ignored. Unlike If… Else which can only have one statement, Elif allows an arbitrary number of Elif statements following If.

Ex14

```
#Ex14

#Program to determine the rate of discount based on price

price = int(input("Enter the price of the item: "))



if price < 100:

        discount = (price * 0.05)

        print ("The discount is ", discount)



elif price < 500:

        discount = (price * 0.1)

        print ("The discount is ", discount)



elif price < 1000:

        discount = (price * 0.2)

        print ("The discount is ", discount)
```

```
else:

        discount = (price * 0.25)

        print ("The discount is ", discount)


print ("The final price of the item is ", price - discount)
```

4.5 Nested IF Statements

In situations where you want to write a program that checks for another condition after a condition is resolved to be True, you can use a nested IF construct. The nested if has the If… Elif…. Else construct within other If… Elif… Else constructs.

Ex15

```
#Ex15

#A program to check if a number is divisible by 3 and 2

num = int(input("Enter a number to check divisibility: "))


if num % 2 == 0:

        if num % 3 == 0:

                print ("Divisible by 2 and 3")
```

```
    else:
        print ("Divisible by 2 not by 3")
else:
    if num % 3 == 0:
        print ("Divisible by 3 not by 2")
    else:
        print ("Not divisible by 2 not by 3")
```

Run the code above and leave comments to understand how this construct works.

Hour 5: Loops

In the last chapter, we saw how the If statement could be an incredibly useful tool in writing a program with conditions to check. However, the If statement and its variations have a problem in that they are one-time operation statements.

As an example, picture a password entry screen. When an If is used, the user can only enter a correct or incorrect password without the option to return to the previous screen if the password is wrong.

Loops have almost the same type of functionality as the If statements except with the advantage of being able to repeat a block of code until you break the cycle. In the example above, with a good loop statement, the user would be taken back to the password screen when they enter an incorrect password instead of just ending the program. A loop can take the user back to the input statement to start a process over.

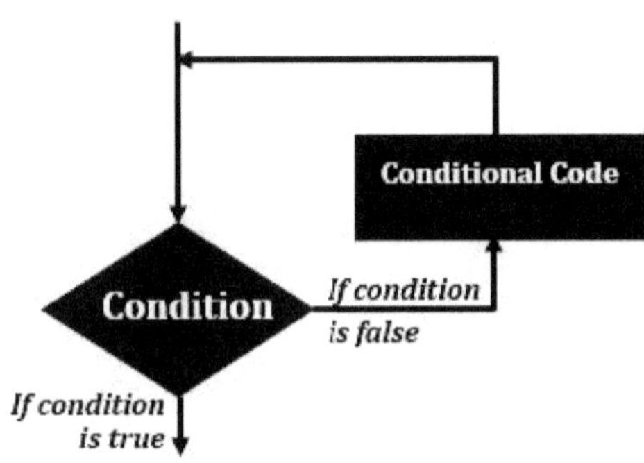

Fig 5: Loop

5.1 The while loop

A while loop statement repeatedly executes a statement or a block of indented code as long as a given condition is true.

Let us begin this section with a simple program. Write the following code and run it, then try to understand what is happening:

Ex16

```
#Ex16

x = 0



while (x < 10):

    x = x + 1

    print (x)
```

You should see a result like this when you run Ex16.py script:

```
1

2

3

4

5

6
```

```
7

8

9

10
```

Here is an explanation of what this short code does:

```
x = 0                        #x now equals 0



while (x < 10):     #As long as the value of x is less than 10, do this:

    x = x + 1        #Add 1 to the value of x

    print (x)                #Display the new value of x and return to first indent.
```

To put it in a simple language you will remember, this is how you write the While loop:

```
while [enter the condition that the loop proceeds]:

        [what is done in the loop]

        [what is done in the loop]

[the code here will not be looped because it is not indented.]
```

Ex17

```
#Ex17
```

```
#Countdown from x to 0

x = int(input("Enter a value between 1 and 10: "))

while x != 0:
        print (x)
        x = x - 1
        print ("The countdown is at ", x)
print ("Countdown ended at 0")
```

Use # comments to explain what each line of the code above does.

5.1.1 Else Statement with While

The Else that we used with IF statement is also used when working with loops. When the Else statement is used with the While loop, the statement after it is excluded when the statement returns Boolean value false.

In the next exercise, you will use Else with the While statement to understand how it works.

Ex18

```
#Ex18

#Countdown from any number greater than 3

x = int(input("Enter a number greater than 3: "))
```

```
while x > 3:
        x = x - 1
        print ("The count is ", x)
else:
        print ("The count is less than 3")
```

It is advisable that you use the while loop sparingly while developing Python programs. The for loop that we will look at next is the more preferred loop to use in most situations.

5.2 The for loop

The For loop requires some repeatable objects like a set or list to execute a sequence of statements and abbreviate the code that handles the loop variable.

Example:

```
x = range (0, 10)
for count in x:
  print (count)
```

The output of this code will look a lot like that in Ex14, yet the program code is very different. The first line introduces the range function which uses two arguments in the format range(start, finish) with start and finish being the first and last numbers in range.

Another way we could have written that code is:

```
for x in range(10):

   print (x)
```

The range() function allows the program to access a set of items efficiently. It executes a loop that runs a fixed number of times when used with the For statement. When the Start value is not declared, the program index begins at 0.

Ex19

```
#Ex19

fruits = ["Apples", "Mangoes", "Peaches", "Oranges", "Bananas"]



for fruit in fruits:

        print (fruit)
```

As we saw earlier, the For statement is an iterator based loop that steps through items in a list, tuples, string, or dictionary keys and other iterable data structures. In this case, the program assigns the list in fruits variable indexes beginning at 0 and follows a sequence of the items in this syntax:

```
for <variable> in <sequence>:

        <statements>
```

5.2.1 Else Statement with For Loop

Just like with the while loop, we can use Else with the For loop. In this case, the else statement is executed when the For loop has exhausted iterating the list of items. Note that the else statement in the For loop is only executed when the For loop terminates normally and not when it encounters a break (discussed below).

The syntax takes this form:

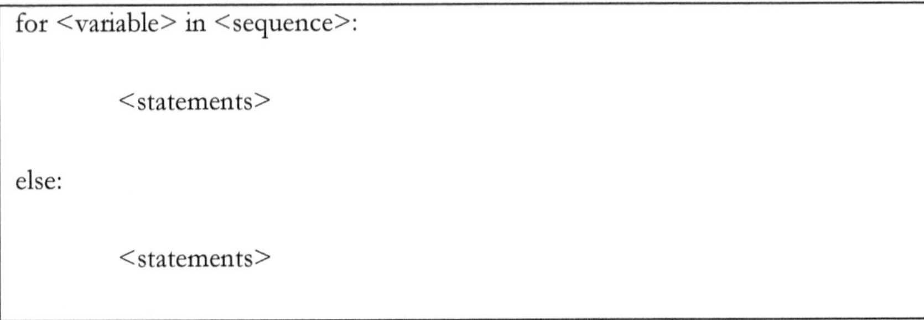

```
for <variable> in <sequence>:

        <statements>

else:

        <statements>
```

Ex20

```
#Ex20

numbers=[1,3,45,49,48,69,37,21,71,41,31]



for num in numbers:

        if num %2 == 0:

                print ("The list contains an even number")

                break

else:
```

```
        print ("The list does not contain even numbers")
```

Find out what happens when you edit out the even number 48 in the numbers list above and run the code.

The program should display "The list does not contain even numbers."

5.4 Loop Control Statements

When you want to change execution from a normal sequence in a loop, you use loop control statements. Python supports pass, break, and continue loop control statements. Let us explore what purpose each of these statements serves.

5.4.1 Pass statement

When a statement is required to syntactically change the execution of a loop without the use of code or command, the pass statement is what you would use. It is a null operation, which means that nothing happens when it is executed. The pass statement is very useful in situations where the code will eventually run but its condition has not yet been met.

Ex21

```
#Ex21

numbers = [3,5,2,7,0,4,3,8,10]

for number in numbers:

        if number == 0:
```

```
                pass

                print ("Pass 0")

        print ("Current number is: ", number)

print ("Bye!")
```

5.4.2 Break statement

The break statement terminates the loop and transfers the next execution to the statement immediately following the loop. This statement is used for premature termination of a loop. After the loop is abandoned, the execution of the next statement is resumed.

Here is a flow diagram showing how the broken syntax works in Python.

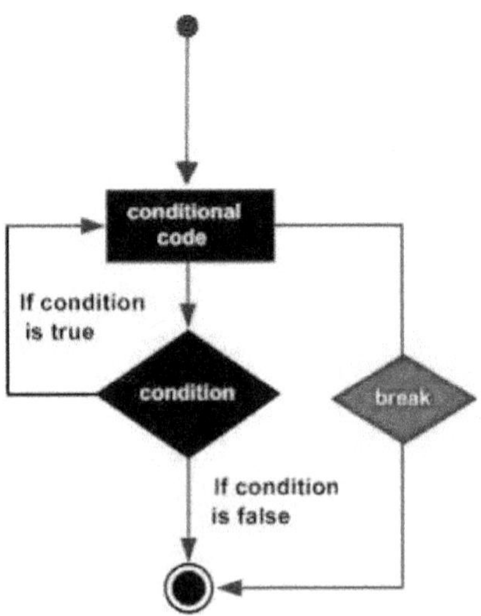

Fig 6: How the break statement works in a loop

The most common use of the break statement us when an external condition that requires a hasty exit is triggered. The break statement, used in both For and While loops, also stops the execution of the innermost loop in a nested loop and begins executing the next line following the block of code.

Ex22

```
#Ex22

age = int(input("How old are you? "))

dob = 2017 - age

counter = 1



while age < 0 or age >130:

        print ("Attempt {0}: Age not valid.".format(counter))

        age = int(input("How old are you? "))

        counter = counter + 1

        if counter >=5:

                age = 0

                break

print ("You used {0} chances to enter your age.".format(counter))

if age == 0:

        print ("You have failed to enter a valid age.")

else:
```

```
print ("You are aged {0}. You were born in ".format(age), dob )
```

In this exercise, the program expects the user to enter his/her age in years and only allows five attempts. The age must be between 0 and 130. The counter records the number of invalid entries, and when it gets to 5, it sets the age as 0 and breaks the loop. When the loop is broken, the very next print statement is executed. If the circuit is not broken, the block after Else is run.

5.4.3 Continue statement

The continue statement causes the loop to skip the remaining part of the block of code and immediately retests the condition before the reiteration.

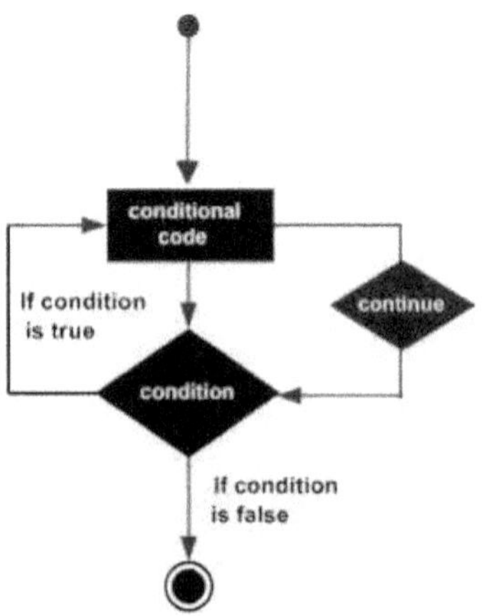

Fig 7: Chart of the Continue statement in a loop.

This statement can be used in both for and while loops.

Ex23

```
#Ex23

while True:

    num = int(input("Enter a positive number to proceed or 0 to exit: "))

    if num < 0:

        print ("Please enter a positive number only.")

        continue

    elif num == 0:

        print ("Exiting program...")

        break

    num_cube = (num ** 3)

    print ("The cube of {0} is {1}.".format (num, num_cube))

print ("Operation completed.")
```

This exercise combines the continue and break loop control expressions, albeit in different blocks of code. Can you explain what they do?

5.5 Indentation

For a code you write to be executed right, all the conditions must be met, including proper indentation. This is particularly important when it comes to loops and iteration. For instance, to loop five lines of code using the while loop, all the five lines must be indented by four spaces or one tab about the beginning of the loop statement.

This is a vital programming practice no matter what language you use. Python requires that you properly indent your code, otherwise your program will encounter errors. In the example below, notice how uniform the indentation is and try to figure out which lines are related.

Ex24

```
#Ex24

x = int(input("Enter a number to test: "))

while x > 0:

    print (x)

    if x > 5:

        print ("The number is greater than 5.")

    elif x % 2 == 0:

        print ("This is an even number.")

        print ("It is also 5 or smaller.")

    else:

        print ("This number is greater than 5.")

        print ("It is also an odd number.")

    x = x - 1

    print ("The value of x is now less by 1.")

print ("The number is greater than 0!")
```

Hour 6: Functions

If you are new to software development, you will be surprised by just how much source code of a program is general and re-usable. Copy-pasting is a very common practice in programming because many functions are similar and instead of re-inventing the wheel each time you write a program, you can just use what someone else has invented.

These include verifying that certain numbers or data types are acceptable if a string fits a particular requirement, or that a print statement works well with a general data structure.

In python, the section of code you would copy whole because it runs independently is called a function. We can define a function as a block of organized and reusable code that performs a single distinct but related action. Functions make your code modular and reusable. Python provides a built-in function such as print (""), but you will also learn to create yours, called user-defined functions.

6.1 Defining a Function

Here are five simple rules you must follow when defining functions in Python:

1. A function block begins with the keyword def followed by the name of the function and parentheses ().
2. The first statement in a function can be an optional statement such as doc string or the documentation string of the function.
3. The code block within the function is indented and begins with a colon (:)
4. Use return [expression] to exit a function, with the option to pass back the expression to the caller.

5. If the function has arguments or input parameters, they should be placed within the parentheses. Parameters can also be defined inside the parentheses.

Without specifying functions, your code would be very repetitive and clumsy. Programmers do not like to repeat things when they do not have to, and considering computers were made just to handle repetitive tasks; it is expected that you use functions to minimize it.

Syntax

```
def functionname(parameters):

        "function_docstring"

        function_suite

        return [expression]
```

Parameters have a positional behavior by default and should be informed in the same order they are defined.

```
numbers = input("Enter two numbers separated by a comma: ")

list = numbers.split(",")

highest = max (list)

print ("The highest value is ", highest)
```

In the above example, we use an inbuilt function called max that finds the maximum value from two or more numbers. This program asks the user to enter several numbers separated by commas then creates a list out of them.

The max function finds the maximum number and assigns variable highest before displaying it.

In Ex25, our task is to define our own function to replace Max above. We will call it MyMax.

Ex25

```
#Ex25

def MyMax (firstnumber, secondnumber):

        if firstnumber > secondnumber:

                return firstnumber

        else:

                return secondnumber



numbers = input("Enter two numbers separated by a comma: ")

list = numbers.split(",")



firstnumber = list[0]

secondnumber = list[1]



result = MyMax(firstnumber, secondnumber)

print (result, "is the greater of the two numbers.")
```

6.2 Calling a Function

When you define a function, you give it a name and specify the parameters that are required for the function to run as well as the structures of its code. After you finalize the basic structure of the function, you will be able to execute it by calling it directly from the Python prompt or another function.

Ex26

```
#Ex26

def cubed(x):

    y = x ** 3

    return y



a = int(input("Enter a number to cube: "))

result = cubed(a)

print ("The result of ", str(a), " cubed is ", str(result))
```

In Ex26, just after the return statement, the program asks the user to enter a number to find a cube for. The number a is 'cubed' as per the cubed function we defined and its result, which is represented by y in the function, is printed out as a string.

You can substitute the expression return with any Python expression and even avoid creating the variable y to represent the answer to leave on return x ** 3 and the program will work just the same (try it).

However, it is a good programming practice to use temporary variables such as y in our defined function to make it easy to debug the program later. Such temporary variables are called local variables.

6.3 Time-saving functions

One of the best things about functions is that they make it possible (and easier) to write an efficient code that you can reuse over and over. For instance, if you write a function that verifies data the user enters, you can use it in the future when you create a program that requires data verification to work.

Before you create a function, you should first find out what its inputs and outputs are. In our case, we know that the user enters an integer as input and gets the output as a string of the cubed number. If our function was efficient enough, it would also verify that the right data is entered (for instance entering alphabetical characters will cause a ValueError.

When you create a function, the best way to maximize its value is to make it time-saving. This means you should be able to tweak the function slightly, if at all, when you want to fit it in another script in the future.

6.4 Pass by reference vs. value

One thing that makes how Python treats function parameters different from standard variables is that its function parameters are passed by value. All parameters (arguments) in Python are passed by reference, meaning that when the value of a parameter the function refers to changes, the change will also be reflected in the calling function. Function parameters are sacred. When a parameter refers to an integer, the function provides a copy of the value of the variable, not access to the variable itself. Let us look at how this works in Ex27.

Ex27

```
#Ex27

def listchange(fruits):

	"This changes the list to this function."

	print ("Parameter values before change: ", fruits)

	fruits[2] = "Vegetable"

	print ("Parameter values after change: ", fruits)

	return



#Now to call the listchange function



fruitslist = input("Enter fruit names separated by commas: ")

fruits = fruitslist.split(",")

listchange(fruits)



print ("Values outside function: ", fruits)
```

Here is what you should see when you run Ex26. In this demo, I used examples Apple, Mango, Peach, and Orange.

```
C:\Python35-32\Exfiles>python ex27.py
```

```
Enter fruit names separated by commas: Apple, Mango, Peach, Orange

Parameter values before change: ['Apple', ' Mango', ' Peach', ' Orange']

Parameter values after change: ['Apple', ' Mango', 'Vegetable', ' Orange']

Values outside function: ['Apple', ' Mango', 'Vegetable', ' Orange']
```

In this demonstration, we have maintained the reference of the passed object while appending a value in the same object. You will notice that the function modifies the third item in the list by replacing it with "Vegetable" value that is retained outside the function.

Let us do another example where an argument is passed by reference, and the reference overwritten inside the function.

Ex28

```
#Ex28

def AgeChanger(ages):

        "This changes a passed list to this function"

        ages = [18,21,34] # This assigns new references to ages

        print ("Values inside the function: ", ages)

        return



#Now call the AgeChanger function

ages = [10,15,20]
```

```
AgeChanger(ages)

print ("Values outside the function: ", ages)
```

When you run this exercise, you should see something like this:

```
C:\Python35-32\Exfiles>python Ex28.py

Values inside the function:  [18, 21, 34]

Values outside the function:  [10, 15, 20]
```

The parameter ages is local to the function AgeChanger function. When you change the ages values within the function, it does not affect ages outside the function, therefore producing nothing.

6.5 Function Arguments

There are several ways you can call a function. You can use the following formal argument types:

- Required arguments
- Keyword arguments
- Default arguments
- Variable-length arguments

6.5.1 Required arguments

These are arguments that are passed to a function in their correct positional order. The number of arguments in the function call must be an exact match with the function definition. Here is a good example.

```
def DisplayMe(str):

   "This prints a passed string into this function"

   print (str)

   return



#Now you can call DisplayMe function

DisplayMe()
```

When you run the example above, you will encounter an error because you have to pass one argument:

TypeError: DisplayMe() missing 1 required positional argument: 'str'

6.5.2 Keyword arguments

Keyword arguments are closely related to function calls. When a keyword argument is used in calling a function, the caller identifies the arguments by the name of the parameter. This makes it possible for you to place arguments out of order or skip them because the interpreter can use the keywords provided to match parameters with values. For instance, we could call the DisplayMe() function like this:

Ex29

```
#Ex29

def DisplayMe(str):

   "This prints a passed string into this function"
```

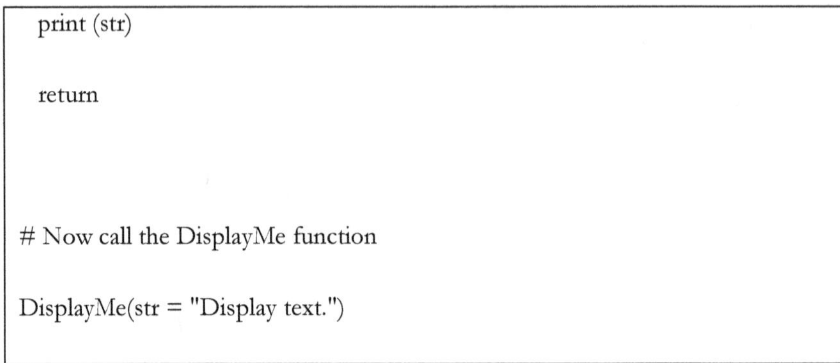

```
  print (str)

  return



# Now call the DisplayMe function

DisplayMe(str = "Display text.")
```

When you run this script you will see this:

```
Display text.
```

To explain this better, we will do an exercise on the same. Keep in mind the order of parameters to see if it matters.

Ex30

```
#Ex30

def showinfo(name, sex):

    "This prints a passed info into the function"

    print ("Name: ", name)

    print ("Sex :", sex)

    return



#Now call the showinfo function

showinfo(sex = "male", name = "John" )
```

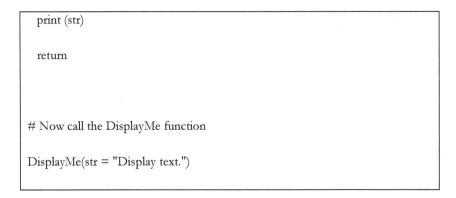

When the Ex30 code is executed, you should see a result like this:

```
C:\Python35-32\Exfiles>python Ex30.py

Name:  John

Sex:  male
```

As you can see, the order of the parameters does not matter when the keyword is used when calling an argument.

6.5.3 Default arguments

A default argument can be defined as an argument that assumes the default value when it is not provided in the function call for the argument. In Ex31, the default age and name argument values are used if not passed.

Ex31

```
#Ex31

def showinfo (name = "Null", age = 20):

        "This prints a passed information into the function"

        print ("Name: ", name)

        print ("Age: ", age)

        return



showinfo(age = 31, name = "Moses")
```

```
showinfo(name = "Sarah") #Default age argument will be used

showinfo(age = 26)      #Default name argument will be used
```

Can you identify situations where default arguments are necessary for Ex31?

6.5.4 Variable-length arguments

A variable-length argument comes in handy when you need to process a function with more arguments than specified in the function definition. Unlike the required and default arguments, the variable-length arguments are not named in the function definition.

The syntax of a function with one-keyword variable arguments looks like this:

```
def function_name([formal_args,] * var_args_tuple):

        "function_docstring"

        function_suite

        return [expression]
```

An asterisk (*) is inserted before the variable name that will hold the values of the non-keyword variable arguments. The variable arguments tuple will remain empty if no new arguments are specified when the function is called.

6.6 The return Statement

The statement return [expression] that we have used throughout this chapter exits the function. A return statement that has no arguments is similar to return None. Ex31 is an example of a function that returns a value.

Ex32

```
#Ex32

def multiply(arg1, arg2):

    "Multiply the parameters and return the product."

    product = arg1 * arg2

    print ("Inside the function: ", product)

    return product



x = int(input("Enter the first number: "))

y = int(input("Enter the second number: "))



#Nowcall the multiply function

answer = multiply(x, y)

print ("Outside the function : ", answer)
```

Hour 7: Dictionaries

Think of a traditional dictionary – the book that provides the definition of English words. The words and their definitions are indexed together in one document, more like a list. Each word and its definition make up a string. The idea behind dictionaries in Python is a lot like this.

On a traditional dictionary, the first word and its definition "a: The first letter of the alphabet" could be assigned index 0 in Python. When referencing a word in the book dictionary, we typically search for a word based on an alphabetical index where instead of searching for index 0 to find the definition of "a," we could refer to it as "index a." Instead of looking at index 0 in the dictionary to find what we want, we look for index a. Instead of dictionary[0], we use dictionary["a"]. Get it?

7.1 Keys and Values of the Dictionary

The idea behind the dictionary in Python is to retrieve values based on more meaningful keys rather than just use a collection of numbers. Dictionaries are in many cases more useful to use than lists, which use numerical indexes to provide access to values. Note, though, that both lists and dictionaries are very helpful in different cases, but you must know their differences to apply them right.

The key and the value of a dictionary is separated by a colon (:), the items are separated by commas (,), and the whole dictionary is enclosed in curly braces ({}). A dictionary called MyDict would look like this:

```
MyDict = {'Name': 'Waldo', 'Age': 25, 'Sex': 'Male', 'Location': 'Italy'}
```

You can also create a similar dictionary like this:

```
MyDict = {

'Name': 'Waldo',

'Age': 25,

'Sex': 'Male',

'Location': 'Italy'

}
```

In a dictionary, keys must be unique while values may not. Keys must also be of immutable data types such as numbers, strings, or tuples but values may not

7.2 Accessing Values in Dictionary

You are already familiar with how to access values in a list using square brackets enclosing an index value, accessing dictionary elements should be a piece of cake because they are pretty much the same thing. Here is a simple example on how to access values in a dictionary:

Ex33

```
#Ex33

MyDict = {'Name': 'Waldo', 'Age': 25, 'Sex': 'Male', 'Location': 'Italy', 'Occupation':'Carpenter'}

print ("I am", MyDict['Name'], "a", MyDict['Age'], MyDict['Sex'], MyDict['Occupation'], "from", MyDict['Location'])
```

Write the above code in your text editor and run it. You should see something like this:

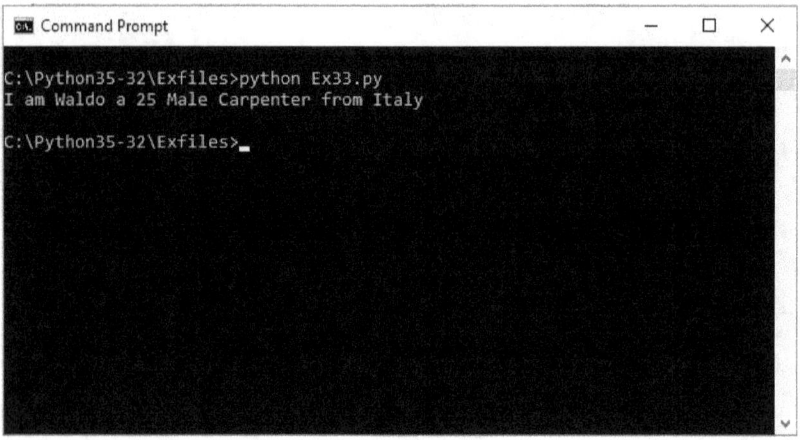

```
Command Prompt

C:\Python35-32\Exfiles>python Ex33.py
I am Waldo a 25 Male Carpenter from Italy

C:\Python35-32\Exfiles>_
```

What happens when you try to access a data item using a key that is not included in the dictionary? Let us try it with the example above and see what error we get.

```
#Ex33

MyDict = {'Name': 'Waldo', 'Age': 25, 'Sex': 'Male', 'Location': 'Italy', 
'Occupation':'Carpenter'}

print ("I am", MyDict['Name'], "a", MyDict['Age'], MyDict['Sex'], 
MyDict['Occupation'], "from", MyDict['Location'], MyDict['Continent'])
```

You should get the error KeyError: 'Continent' when you run the code above. This essentially means that the key does not exist.

7.3 Updating the Dictionary

You can update the dictionary by adding new entries or key-value pairs or modifying or deleting existing entries. In Ex33, we will put each of these in practice to understand how they work.

7.3.1 Modifying Dictionary Elements

Ex34

```
#Ex34

MyDict = {'Name': 'Waldo', 'Age': 25, 'Sex': 'Male', 'Location': 'Italy'}



name = str(input("Enter a new name: "))

age = int(input("Enter your age: "))

location = str(input("Where are you? "))



MyDict['Name'] = name

MyDict['Age'] = age

MyDict['Location'] = location



print ("The new user is", MyDict['Name'], "aged", MyDict['age'], "from",
MyDict['Location']+".")
```

This shortcode has a dictionary with four keys with paired values. It prompts the user for new values stored in variables called name, age, and location then assigns them to the 'Name,' 'age,' and 'Location' keys of the MyDict dictionary.

Can you modify the code to allow the user to enter a new string and modify the 'Sex' value in the dictionary?

7.3.2 Deleting Dictionary Elements

There are functions that you can use to remove the elements of a dictionary individually or erase all the contents at once. You can also use del.dict to delete the entire dictionary. Note that when you delete the dictionary, any references to it or its keys and values will return an exception because the dictionary will no longer exist.

Ex35

```
#Ex35

MyDict = {'Name': 'Waldo', 'Age': 25, 'Sex': 'Male', 'Location': 'Italy'}



print ("List of keys before deletion:",list(MyDict.keys()))



del MyDict['Location']



print ("List of keys after deletion:", list(MyDict.keys()))
```

This code will give you a KeyError: 'Location' when you run it because 'Location' has been removed.

To clear all the entries in the dictionary, dict.clear().

7.4 Properties of Dictionary Keys

There are no restrictions as far as using dictionary values goes. You can use arbitrary objects including standard and user-defined objects. However, when it comes to keys, there are two important rules you must always remember as I mentioned in the introduction:

1. Keys must be unique. You cannot have more than one similar keys in a dictionary.
2. Keys are immutable. You cannot use something like [key] to define a key.

7.5 Built-in Dictionary Functions and Methods

In this section, I will go through a list of the essential functions and approaches built into Python that you can use with dictionaries. I suggest that you study the description of the different methods and functions and apply them to Ex36 then run the code to see what they do.

Ex36

```
#Ex36

GradsList = {'StudentID': 200627,'FirstName': 'Alison','LastName':
'Fairbanks','Email': 'afairbanks@email.com','DOB': 1995,'Sex': 'F','Major':
'Music','Faculty': 'Arts',}
```

For example, to try the len(GradsDict) function, first understand what it does, find out what the output should be, then enter this in your Ex36.py code:

```
#Ex36

GradsDict = {'StudentID': 200627,'FirstName': 'Alison','LastName':
'Fairbanks','Email': 'afairbanks@email.com','DOB': 1995,'Sex': 'F','Major':
'Music','Faculty': 'Arts',}



print ("len(dict):", len(GradsDict))
```

Function	**Description**
len(GradsDict)	This is the length function which gives the number of items in the dictionary.
str(GradsDict)	This gives a printable string representation of the dictionary.
type(variable)	Gives the type of the passed variable. For a dictionary, it returns dictionary type.
Method	**Description**
GradsDict.clear()	Removes all the elements in the dictionary including keys and values.
GradsDict.copy()	Makes a shallow copy of the GradsDict dictionary
GradsDict.fromkeys()	Creates a new dictionary with the GradsDict keys.
GradsDict.get(key, default=None)	For the specified key (e.g.) 'email', returns value. If no value is assigned, it returns default.
GradsDict.items()	Returns the GradsDict (key, value) tuple pairs as a list.
GradsDict.keys()	Returns a list of the GradsDict keys.
GradsDict.setdefault(key, default=None)	Similar to get() except that it sets the GradsDict[key] to default if it is not in the dictionary already
GradsDict.update(GradsDict2)	Takes the key-value pairs of GradsDict2 and adds them to GradsDict
GradsDict.values()	Returns the values of GradsDict dictionary.

Hour 8: Classes

In the introduction to this book, we described Python as an Object Oriented Programming language. This is because Python lets you structure your code in a way that uses modules, classes, and objects with ease. This chapter focuses on helping you master Python's object-oriented setup to create a consistent program that can be run in a 'cleaner' way. You will find out what objects in programming are and how modules and classes are used.

If you find it difficult to grasp these full, do not worry because everyone new to programming struggles at first to understand the plain weird set up that is OOP. In the conclusion of this book, you will find a few recommendations of web resources you can refer to understand the in-depths of OOP fully.

8.1 Overview of Terminologies used in OOP

Class: This is a prototype for an object defined by the user with attributes that characterize an object. The characteristics, in this case, include data members (instance and class variables) and methods.

Object: An object is made up of data members including class variables and instance variables as well as methods that create a unique instance of a data structure defined by its class.

Data member: This is an instance variable or a class variable that stores the data associated with an object and its class.

Class variable: This is a variable that is shared by all the instances of a class. It is defined within a class but outside of any of the class's methods.

Instance variable: This is a variable defined inside a method. An instance variable belongs only to the current class instance.

Instance: An object of a particular class also defined as an object that belongs to a class Circle.

Instantiation: The process of creating an instance of a class.

Inheritance: Inheritance is the process of transferring the characteristics of class to other classes derived from the parent class.

Method: A special form of the function defined within a class definition.

Function overloading: This is when you assign more than one behavior to a function. Function overloading varies with the types of arguments and objects involved.

Operator overloading: This is when more than one function is assigned to an operator.

8.2 Creating Classes

To put it in a way that is easy to understand, a class is a kind of container where you will group all related data and functions to be able to access using a "." (dot) operator.

A new class definition is created using the class statement followed by the name of the class then a colon, like this:

```
class ClassName:

        "class documentation string"

        class_suite
```

The class can also have an optional documentation string right below the definition as shown above and can be accessed using ClassName._doc_.

The class_suite contains all the basic statements that define the class members, functions, and data attributes.

Ex37

```
#Ex37

class MyContacts:

    "Details of my contacts"

    ContCount = 0

    def __init__(self, name, number):

        self.name = name

        self.number = number

        MyContacts.ContCount += 1

    def ContactCount(self):

        print ("Total contacts:", MyContacts.ContCount)



    def ShowContact(self):

        print (self.name, "-", self.number)
```

In this exercise, we have created a class called MyContacts.

- The ContCountvariable is a class variable. Its value is shared with all the instances of the class and can be accessed as MyContacts.ContCount within and outside the class.
- The _init_() method is a unique method also called initialization or the class constructor method. Python calls this method when you create a new instance of the MyContactsclass
- The first argument to each method is self. All other categories are declared like standard functions. You do not need to add the self-argument to the list because Python adds it for you.

8.3 Creating Instance Objects

To create a new instance of a class, first, you call the class using the class name then pass in the arguments that the_init_ method accepts. Let us create an instance object for the class we set up in Ex36. Modify Ex36 by adding the following instance objects:

```
"These create the objects of the MyContacts class"

Contact1 = Mycontacts("Bonny", "0789182733")

Contact2 = MyContacts("Peter", "0739237494")

Contact3 = MyContacts("Janet", "0718297621")
```

Save the new code as Ex38.py. Your exercise code should look like this:

Ex38

```
#Ex38

class MyContacts:
```

```
    "Details of my contacts"

    ContCount = 0



    def __init__(self, name, number):

        self.name = name

        self.number = number

        MyContacts.ContCount += 1



    def ContactCount(self):

        print ("Total contacts:", MyContacts.ContCount)



    def ShowContact(self):

        print (self.name, "-", self.number)



"These create the objects of the MyContacts class"

Contact1 = Mycontacts("Bonny", "0789182733")

Contact2 = MyContacts("Peter", "0739237494")

Contact3 = MyContacts("Janet", "0718297621")
```

8.4 Accessing and Working with Attributes

Attributes are accessed using the dot (.) operator with the object. A class variable is accessed using the class name like this: Contact1.ShowContact().

In Ex38, we are going to access the attributes added in Ex37. Modify the Ex37 code again as shown below and save it as Ex38.py then execute it from the terminal.

Ex39

```
#Ex39

class MyContacts:

        "Details of my contacts"

        ContCount = 0



        def __init__(self, name, number):

                self.name = name

                self.number = number

                MyContacts.ContCount += 1



        def ContactCount(self):

                print ("Total contacts:", MyContacts.ContCount)
```

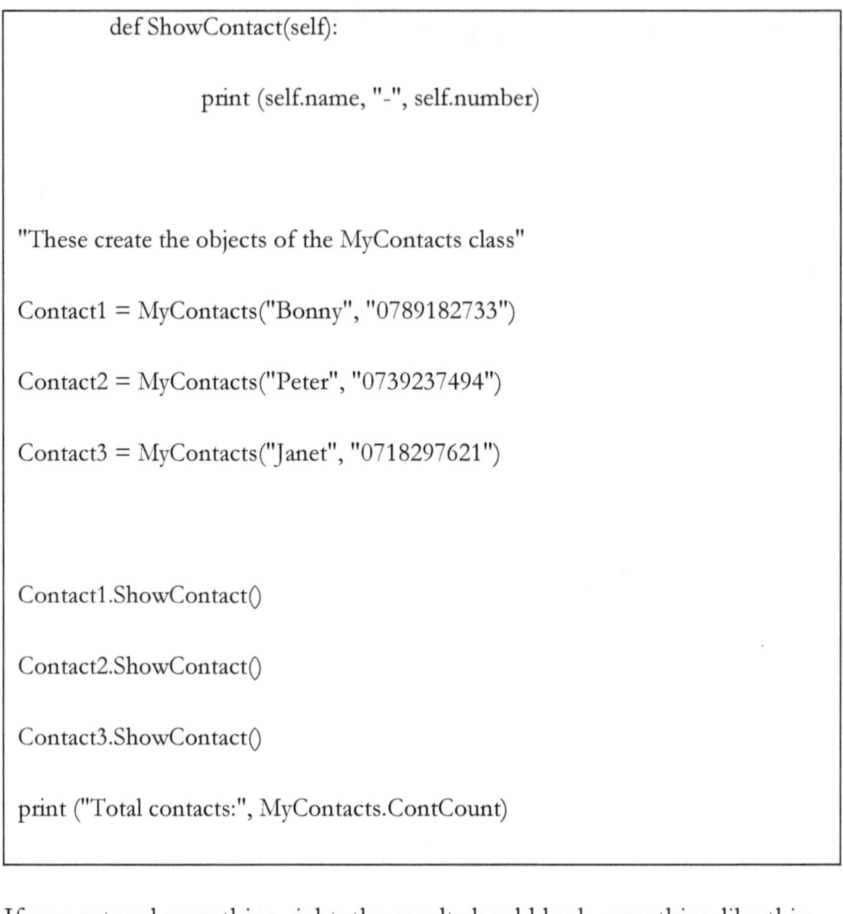

```
        def ShowContact(self):

                print (self.name, "-", self.number)



"These create the objects of the MyContacts class"

Contact1 = MyContacts("Bonny", "0789182733")

Contact2 = MyContacts("Peter", "0739237494")

Contact3 = MyContacts("Janet", "0718297621")



Contact1.ShowContact()

Contact2.ShowContact()

Contact3.ShowContact()

print ("Total contacts:", MyContacts.ContCount)
```

If you entered everything right, the result should look something like this:

```
C:\Python35-32\Exfiles>Python Ex38.py

Bonny - 0789182733

Peter - 0739237494

Janet - 0718297621

Total contacts: 3
```

In Ex40, we will practice adding and modifying attributes.

If you entered everything right, the result should look something like this:

Ex40

```
#Ex40
class MyContacts:
	"Details of my contacts"
	ContCount = 0

	def __init__(self, name, number):
		self.name = name
		self.number = number
		MyContacts.ContCount += 1

	def ContactCount(self):
		print ("Total contacts:", MyContacts.ContCount)

	def ShowContact(self):
		print (self.name, "-", self.number)

"These create the objects of the MyContacts class"
Contact1 = MyContacts("Bonny", "0789182733")
Contact2 = MyContacts("Peter", "0739237494")
Contact3 = MyContacts("Janet", "0718297621")

print ("Original class attributes:")
Contact1.ShowContact()
Contact2.ShowContact()
Contact3.ShowContact()
print ("Total contacts:", MyContacts.ContCount)
```

```
Contact1.name = "Boniface"
Contact2.name = "Nancy"
Contact3.number = "0779204852"


print ("Updated class attributes:")
print ("Total contacts:", MyContacts.ContCount)
Contact1.ShowContact()
Contact2.ShowContact()
Contact3.ShowContact()
```

Here are the functions you can use to add, modify, and delete attributes:

- getattr(obj, name, [default]) is used to access the attribute of an object
- hasattr(obj, name)is used to check if an attribute exists or not.
- setattr(obj, name, value)is used to set an attribute or create one if it does not exist.
- delattr(obj, name)is used to delete an attribute.

8.5 Built-In Class Attributes

Every Python class by default has the following attributes built-in and can be accessed using the dot (.) operator just like any other attribute.

__name__: Class name.

__dict__: Dictionary containing namespace of the class.

__doc__: Class documentation string. If undefined, none.

__module__("__main__"in interactive mode): Module name in which the class is defined.

__bases__: A tuple containing the base classes arranged in order of occurrence in the base class list. This class could be possibly empty.

Let us used these attributes in the code we saved as Ex 38 to see firsthand what they do. Save the code as Ex40 and run it on the terminal.

Ex41

```
#Ex41

class MyContacts:

        "Details of my contacts"

        ContCount = 0



        def __init__(self, name, number):

                self.name = name

                self.number = number

                MyContacts.ContCount += 1



        def ContactCount(self):

                print ("Total contacts:", MyContacts.ContCount)



        def ShowContact(self):

                print (self.name, "-", self.number)
```

```
print ("MyContacts.__doc__:", MyContacts.__doc__)

print ("MyContacts.__name__:", MyContacts.__name__)

print ("MyContacts.__module__:", MyContacts.__module__)

print ("MyContacts.__bases__:", MyContacts.__bases__)

print ("MyContacts.__dict__:", MyContacts.__dict__)
```

8.6 Class Inheritance

You do not need to create a class from scratch every time. If you can derive it from an existing class, list the parent class in parentheses right after the new class name. The child class will inherit the attributes of the parent class, and you will be able to use its attributes just as if they are defined in the child class. A child class will, however, override any data members and methods from the parent class.

Here is the syntax for class inheritance:

You can also derive a class from two or more parent classes as demonstrated in the syntax above. You can use isinstance() or issubclass()to check how two classes and instances relate.

- isinstance(ChildClass, ParentClass)is a Boolean function that will return true if the given child class is a subclass of the parent class.
- issubclass(object, class)is a Boolean function that returns true if the objis an instance of the class or if an instance is a subclass of the class.

8.7 Overriding Methods

You can override the parent class methods when working with a child class especially if you want a different or special functionality in the subclass. Here are some of the generic functionalities that you can override in the subclasses:

__init__ (self [,args...]): This is a constructor with optional arguments.

__del__ (self): Deletes an object.

__repr__ (self): Represents an evaluable string.

__str__ (self): Represents a printable string.

__cmp__ (self, x): Used to compare objects.

8.8 Overloading Operators

If your code will at some point add two-dimensional vectors, you could define the __add__ method in the class to handle vector addition to preventing errors. Here is a demo you can try:

Ex42

```
#Ex42

class NumAdder:

  def __init__(self, x, y):

    self.x = x

    self.y = y
```

```
    def __str__(self):

        return "NumAdder (%d, %d)" % (self.x, self.y)



    def __add__(self, z):

        return NumAdder(self.x + z.x, self.y + z.y)



a1 = NumAdder(5, 7)

a2 = NumAdder(-3, 9)

print (a1 + a2)
```

Hour 9: Files and Exceptions

When your program is running, it stores the data it is working with temporarily in the computer's primary memory. This data is lost when the program ends or the computer powers off. The only way to store data permanently is to save it in a file that is stored in the computer's secondary memory which is typically the hard disk.

9.1 Reading and Writing Files

By default, Python offers basic methods and functions a user needs to manipulate files. Most of these file manipulation processes use the file object. The most important commands that you need to understand how they work and know how to use in this section are:

read(): Accesses the contents of the file. You will learn to assign the contents of the file to a variable.

write(): This method enters data into the file.

readline(): Unlike read, this function reads just one line in the text file.

truncate(): This command empties the content of a text file. Be careful when using truncate on files with vital data.

close(): This closes the file, much like the File > Save process in your text editor/

For the exercises in this hour, we will create a text file in our default save directory (where you save .py files) and give it the name Poem.txt. You can do this right from your text editor.

```
The Dust of Snow



The way a crow

Shook down on me

The dust of snow

From a hemlock tree



Has given my heart

A change of mood

And saved some part

Of a day I had rued.
```

Save the file as Poem.txt.

9.1.1 The read() Method

We use read() to read a string of text or binary data from an open file. The syntax for this method takes this format:

```
fileobject = open(file_name, [access_mode], [buffering])
```

file_name: This string value argument contains the name of the files you want to access.

access_mode: This is an optional parameter that determines the mode in which a file can be opened. The table below summarizes the different modes you should know about.

Mode	Description
r	This is read-only mode. Unless specified, the default mode in which a file is opened is in this mode by default. The file pointer is positioned at the start of the file.
rb	Opens a file in binary format for reading only. The pointer is positioned at the start of the file.
r+	Opens a file for reading and writing in text format. The file pointer positioned at the start of the file.
rb+	Opens a file for reading and writing but in binary format. The file pointer placed at the beginning of the file.
w	Opens a file for writing only and overwrites the file it already exists. If it does not exist a new file for writing is created.
wb	Opens a file for writing only but in binary format and creates one if the file does not exists. Overwrites if the file already exists.
w+	Opens a file ready for reading and writing and overwrites the existing file if it already. If the file does not exist, a new one for reading and writing is created.
wb+	Opens a file in binary format for reading and writing and overwrites the existing one if already exists. If it does not, a new one ready for reading and writing is created.
a	Opens a file in append mode. The pointer is positioned at the end of the file if it exists. If the file does not exist, a new one for writing is created.
ab	Opens a file in binary format in append mode. The pointer is positioned at the end of the file if it exists. If the file does not exist, a new one for writing is created.
a+	Opens a file for reading and appending in the append mode. The file pointer is at the end of the file if it exists. If it does not exist, a one is created for reading and writing.
ab+	Opens a file in binary format for reading and appending in append mode. The pointer is positioned at the end of the file if the file exists. A new file is created for reading and writing in if the file does not exist.

file_name: This string value argument contains the name of the files you want to access.

Buffering: If the value of buffering is set to 0, no buffering will take place. If set to 1, the program performs line buffering when accessing the file. If the buffering value is specified as an integer greater than 1, buffering is performed with the specified buffer size. If the value specified is negative, the system's default buffer size is used.

Ex43

Start a new file on your text file and enter the following code for Ex43:

```
#Ex43

text = open("Poem.txt", "r")

MyPoem = text.read(16); #Reads the first 16 bytes in the text and assigns variable MyPoem

print ("Read String is:", MyPoem)



text.close() #Closes the opened file
```

Run Ex42 and see what happens. This is what you should see:

```
C:\Python35-32\Exfiles>Python Ex43.py

Read String is: The Dust of Snow
```

When you open a file using Python's inbuilt open() function, a file object will be created which you can use to call support methods it is associated with.

9.1.2 The write() Method

When you need to write a string of data into an open file, you use the write() method. Note that strings in Python may contain binary data and not just text. You should also remember that this method does not ('\n') character to the end of the string. This character adds a new line to the end of the string such that the next string will be displayed in a new line.

The syntax for write() looks like this:

```
fileObject.write(string);
```

Ex44

```
#Ex44

MyFile = open("MyFile.txt", "w")

MyFile.write("Poem: The Dust of Snow.\n By Robert Frost\n");



print ("File created and saved.\n")



MyFile.close() #Close the opened file



MyText = open("MyFile.txt", "r+")

MyPoem = MyText.read(42);
```

```
print ("File content: \n" + MyPoem)



MyText.close()
```

The above exercise has two unique processes. Can you identify which one writes the file then closes it and which one opens and prints it show what string was written to the file MyFile.txt?

9.2 File Positions

If you wish to specify where in the file you would like to read or write text, the tell() method will show you the current position in bytes about the beginning of the file.

The seek(offset, [from]) method is then used to change the file position, with the offset argument indicating the number of bytes by which the position is moved. The [from]argument references the position from which the bytes are moved.

If the from argument is set to 0, the beginning of the file will be the reference position, and if it is 1, the current position will be the reference position. If it is set to 2, the end of the file will be the reference position in the method.

Let us try out these file position commands in Ex45 using the MyFile.txt file we created in Ex44.

Ex45

```
#Ex45

MyText = open("MyFile.txt", "r+")
```

```
text = MyText.read(50)



print ("String content:", text)



position = MyText.tell(); #To check the pointer position

print ("The current position is", position)



position = MyText.seek(0, 0) #Move the pointer to the begining of the file

print ("\n New position is", position)



MyText.close()
```

9.3 Renaming and Deleting Files

The OS module of Python offers various methods that you can use to perform various file processing and manipulation operations including renaming and deleting files. However, to call the functions of this module, you will first need to import it using import os.

9.3.1 Renaming files using the rename() method

The rename() method requires two arguments: the current name of the file to rename and the new filename to rename to. The syntax goes something like this:

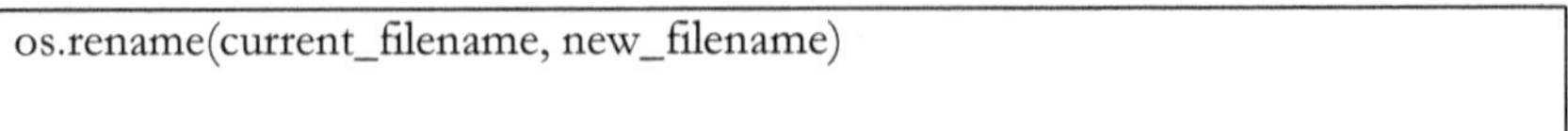

```
os.rename(current_filename, new_filename)
```

In Ex46, let us rename the MyFile.txt file we created to MyPoem.txt.

Ex46

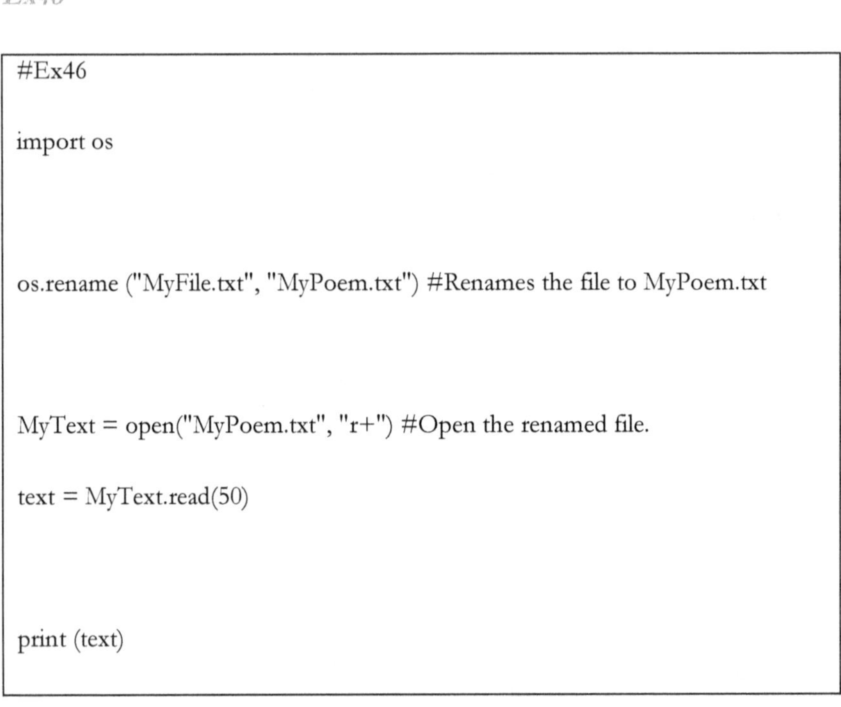

```
#Ex46

import os



os.rename ("MyFile.txt", "MyPoem.txt") #Renames the file to MyPoem.txt



MyText = open("MyPoem.txt", "r+") #Open the renamed file.

text = MyText.read(50)



print (text)
```

9.3.2 Deleting files using the remove() method

The os.remove() method is used to delete files. The argument required by the method is the name of the file to be removed. It looks like this:

```
os.remove(file_name)
```

We will go ahead and delete the MyFile.txt file we created in Ex44 in Ex47. If the file no longer exists in your folder, you can create one and give it the exact similar name or only run Ex43.py again to create it.

Ex47

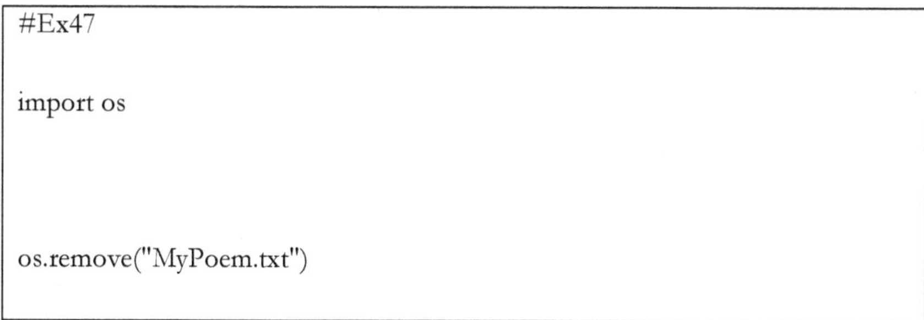

```
#Ex47

import os



os.remove("MyPoem.txt")
```

Remember to restore the deleted file MyPoem.txt because we will need it in the next exercise.

9.4 File and Directory Related Methods

There are countless resources on the internet where you can learn and practice a broad range of methods you can use to manipulate and handle files and directories. These resources cover:

- OS Object Methods: This offers ways to process files and folders (directories).
- File Object Methods: The file object provides many functions used to manipulate files.

When you pursue learning Python beyond this stage, you will learn how to manipulate and work with directories.

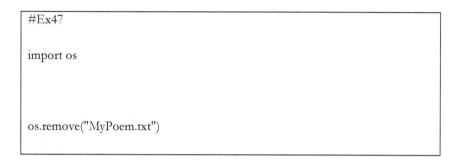

Hour 10: Errors and Exceptions

Errors that happen during the execution of program code are called exceptions. To the average software user, an exception is an instance where a program does not conform to the general and defined rules as expected.

An error is resolved by saving the status of the execution when the error occurred and interrupted the normal program flow. An exception handler is a piece of code that is used to determine the type and cause of an exception or error.

Depending on the type of error encountered, the exception handler can fix the problem encountered and allow the program to resume normal flow or it will stop prompt the user for data or instructions before resumption.

Python comes with two vital tools used to handle any unexpected errors in the code and to debug it: They are:

1. Exception handlers
2. Assertions

When a script in Python raises an exception, it must be handled immediately; otherwise, the program will terminate and quit.

10.1 Exception Handling

In Python, a code that harbors the risk of an exception is embedded in a try block and caught by an except keyword. Python allows you to create a custom exception, even using the raise statement to force a specified exception to occur.

10.1.1 Table of Standard Exceptions

Before we can learn how to use exception handlers to deal with errors in code, let us first discover what the errors we should expect to encounter are and what they mean. You can always refer to this table to find what caused a mistake you encounter.

Exception	**Description**
Exception	This is the base class for all exceptions.
Attribute Error	This exception is raised by a failure of attribute assignment or reference.
ArithmeticError	This is the base class for all errors in numeric calculation.
StopIteration	Occurs when an iterator's `next()` method does not point to any object.
SystemExit	Exception caused by the `sys.exit()` function.
StandardError	This is the base class for all built-in exceptions except SystemExit and StopIteration.
OverflowError	Encountered when a calculation exceeds the maximum limit for a numeric type.
FloatingPointError	Raised when there is a failure of a floating point calculation.
ZeroDivisonError	Occurs when there is division or modulo by zero on any numeric types.
AssertionError	Occurs when there is a failure of the Assert statement.
EOFError	Raised when the end of file is reached and there is no input from `input()` function.
ImportError	Occurs as a result of an import statement failure.
KeyboardInterrupt	Encountered when the user interrupts the execution of the program execution, often by pressing *Ctrl+C*.
LookupError	This is the base class for all lookup errors.

IndexError	Error occurs when an index is not found in a specified sequence.
KeyError	Occurs when a specified key is not found in the dictionary.
NameError	Occurs when an identifier is not found in a specified namespace.
UnboundLocalError	Occurs when the program tries to access a local variable in a method or function without a value assigned to it.
EnvironmentError	This is the base class for all exceptions occurring outside the Python environment.
IOError	Occurs when an input or output operation fails.
OSError	Triggered by Operating system-related errors.
SyntaxError	Occurs when there is an error in the code syntax.
IndentationError	Caused by improper indentation.
SystemError	Caused by an internal problem with the interpreter.
SystemExit	Encountered when the interpreter is terminated using the `sys.exit()` function.
TypeError	Raised when an operation encounters a data type different from the specified.
ValueError	Encountered when arguments have invalid values specified despite the built-in functions having the right argument types.
NotImplementedError	Triggered when an abstract method that is expected to run in an inherited class is not implemented.

10.1.2 Exception Handling Syntax

If you suspect that a block of code in your script could raise an exception, it is a good practice to place the suspicious code inside a try: block and below it an except: statement that will handle the error correctly. The syntax of the code would look something like this:

```
try:

        Enter your code here;

except PossibleException1:

        If there is PossibleException1, then run this code

except PossibleException2:

        If there is PossibleException2, then run this code

else:

        If there is no exception then run this code.
```

Note that:

- A single try: the statement can have one or more except statements. This is important when you are trying to handle possible multiple errors that you suspect your one block of code could rise.
- It is a good practice to provide a generic except clause that handles any and all exceptions.
- The else: clause is optional. Its code executes only when there are no exceptions raised by the try: block code. You can place the code that does not need the protection of the try: block in the else: block.

In Ex48, we will try to open the file MyFile.txt which we do not have permission to write, to raise an exception.

Ex48

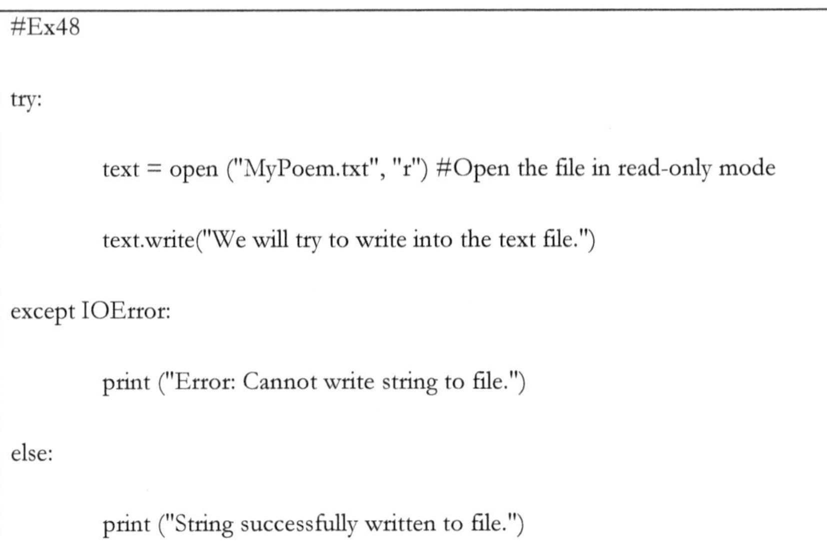

```
#Ex48

try:

        text = open ("MyPoem.txt", "r") #Open the file in read-only mode

        text.write("We will try to write into the text file.")

except IOError:

        print ("Error: Cannot write string to file.")

else:

        print ("String successfully written to file.")
```

When you run the code above on your terminal, you should see this:

```
C:\Python35-32\Exfiles>python Ex48.py

Error: Cannot write string to file.
```

Now, try eliminating the error by opening the file in read and write mode then run it. What does it print?

Hint: Change "r" to "r+".

Let us try another example. In Ex49, the program expects the user to enter an integer as the value of n. It should generate an error when the input is a string instead. We will raise a ValueError then use the try: exception handling to resolve it.

Ex49

```
#Ex49

while True:

        try:

                n = int(input("Please enter your age:"))

                break

        except ValueError:

                print ("Your age must be an integer. Try again.")

print ("You are aged", n, "years.")
```

This script contains a loop that only breaks when the user enters a valid integer.

If you have a code that must execute whether an exception is raised in the try block or not, you can use the finally: clause. The syntax would look like this: use the finally: clause. The syntax would look like this:

```
try:

        Enter your code here;

        In case of an exception, this block is skipped.

finally:

        This block will ALWAYS be executed.
```

Let us write a script example that puts the try: and finally: clauses in use.

Ex50

```
#Ex50

try:

        text = open("MyPoem.txt", "w") #Open the file in write-only mode.

        text.write ("Dust of Snow by Robert Frost")

finally:

        print ("Error: Cannot find the file or read the data.")
```

Note: You cannot use the else: clause along with the finally: clause.

When there is an exception in the try: block, the execution will be passed to the finally: block immediately. The exception will be raised again after all the statements in the finally: block are executed then handled by the except statement if it is present in a following higher layer of the try: then except statement. Let us try it in Ex50 by writing a script that finds the reciprocal of a number entered by the user.

Ex51

```
#Ex51

try:

        x = float(input("Enter a number: "))

        reciprocal = 1.0 / x
```

```
except ValueError:

        print ("You did not enter a valid integer or float.")

except ZeroDivisionError:

        print ("Cannot divide by 0!")

finally:

        print ("This prints whether there is an exception or not.")
```

10.2 Assertions

In Python, an assertion is a tool that you use to find bugs faster and with less pain. You can turn it on before use and turn it off after you are finished testing your code. It will test an expression and raise an exception if the result is FALSE. It is a good practice to place the assert statement at the beginning of a function to ensure an input is valid and after a function to validate the output.

10.2.1 The asset statement

Python evaluates accompanying expressions to determine if they are TRUE or FALSE when it encounters the assert statement. If the result is false, the AssertionError exception is raised. The syntax for this statement is:

```
assert Expression[Argument]
```

Ex52

```
#Ex52

def CtoF_Converter(Temp):

        "Convert degrees C to F"

#

        assert (Temp >= -273.15), "Cannot be colder than absolute zero!"

        return 9.0 / 5.0 * Temp + 32



C = float(input("Enter temperature in Celsius: "))

F = CtoF_Converter(C)



print (C, "degrees Celcius is", F, "degrees Fahrenheit.")
```

If you run the Ex52.py and enter a number less than 273.15, you should encounter an assertion error akin to this:

```
C:\Python35-32\Exfiles>python Ex52.py

Enter temperature in Celsius: -280

Traceback (most recent call last):

  File "Ex51.py", line 17, in <module>

    F = CtoF_Converter(C)
```

```
  File "Ex51.py", line 13, in CtoF_Converter

    assert (Temp >= -273.15), "Cannot be colder than absolute zero!"

AssertionError: Cannot be colder than absolute zero!
```

Hour 11: Testing Your Code

Testing your code is one of the most important steps of developing a functional program. In fact, it is typically considered a good practice to write testing code than running it in parallel to your primary code. This method is widely used by developers across the development sphere as it helps developers define the precise intent of their code and to create software with more decoupled architecture.

11.1 General rules of testing Python code

Here are the ten commandments of testing your code in Python.

1. The testing unit of your code should focus on a tiny bit of functionality and should prove it correct.
2. Each testing unit should be completely independent. It should be able to run alone within the test suite regardless of the order it is called. The setup() and teardown() methods can be used to load new datasets and cleanup after testing.
3. Always try to make tests run fast to avoid slowing down the entire development. If testing takes longer because of complex data structure it must process, the test units can be run in separate suites.
4. Practice using your tools to run only tests or test cases then runs them when developing functions inside modules frequently, ideally, automatically every time you save your code.
5. Make it a habit of running the full test suite prior to and after every coding session to be sure that noting is broken in the code before starting or and when ending the session.
6. Put in place a hook that runs all tests before pushing the code to a shared depository if working on the collaborative code.

7. If your development session is interrupted, make a point of writing a broken unit test about what you intend to develop next to know where to start when you resume the next session.
8. The first step in debugging your code should be writing a new test that pinpoints the bug. This is not always the easiest thing to do, but this will help you catch those elusive bugs faster and more comprehensively in your code.
9. Write long descriptive names for your testing functions because unlike regular code, and the unit test code is never called explicitly.
10. Every unit test must have a clear purpose of making it helpful. When something goes wrong, or you have to make some changes, you will rely on the testing suite to make modifications or modify certain behaviors.

11.2 unittest

unittest is a test module that comes with the Python standard library. You can create a test case on unittest by subclassing the unittest.TestCase as shown in exercise 53 syntax code below.

Ex53

```
#Ex53

import unittest



def counter(x):

    return x + 1
```

```
class MyTest(unittest.TestCase):

    def test(self):

        self.assertEqual(counter(4), 5)
```

unittest comes with its test discovery capabilities.

11.3 Doctest

A doctest module searches the code for text that looks like interactive sessions in docstrings then executes them to verify that they execute exactly as shown. Unlike proper unit tests, doctests have different uses and are usually not as detailed. Because of this, doctests do not typically catch obscure regression bugs and special cases.

Doctests are however very useful used as expressive documentation of the main use cases of modules and its components. They should, however, run automatically each time a full test suite is run. Here is an example of how a doctest syntax looks like.

Ex54

```
#Ex54

def square(x):

        """Return the square of x.

        >>> square(3)

        9
```

```
        >>> square(-3)

        9

        """

        return x * x



if __name__ == '__main__':

    import doctest

    doctest.testmod()
```

11.4 Tools

In this section, I will mention several popular testing tools that you will learn to install and use when you get to learning advanced testing of Python code.

11.4.1 py.test

The py.test is an alternative to the standard unittest module that Python comes with. It is a fully-featured and extensible testing tool that has very simple syntax. Creating a test suite using py.test is as easy as writing a module with several functions.

11.4.2 Nose

Nose is a tool that extends unittest so as to make testing code easier. The nose offers automatic test discovery to save the programmer the hassle of having to create test suites manually. It also comes with multiple plugins with extra features such as coverage reporting, test selection, and xUnit compatible test output.

11.4.3 tox

Tox is a versatile tool that you can use to automate the Python test environment management and even test multiple interpreter configurations. This tool lets you configure complex multi-parameter test matrices using a simple ini-style config file.

11.4.4 Unittest2

This is a backport of Python's unittest module. It features an improved API as well as better aassertions over the original unittest.

11.4.5 mock

unittest.mock features many library tools that you can use to test your Python code. Mock allows you to replace parts of the system you are testing with mock objects and test code by making assertions on how they have been used. It is available in the standard Python library starting with Python 3.3.

Hour 12: Conclusion & Further Reading

Over 50 programs of Python written so far since the first Hello World program about 12 hours, ago (hours of study) and you have become an even better and experienced program. If you followed every step of this eBook so far, you have earned the bragging rights to call yourself a programmer. You started from scratch (like everyone should) and perhaps with no prior experience in programming, can now speak regarding functions, classes, IOError, and much more geeky terms.

This short eBook is compressed to keep it concise and practical. You have so far learned how to tell the computer to do all kinds of things, process text, save your information, and saved processes you have personalized to do exactly what you want. The magic has been to learn how to tell the computer what to do, a skill most people still perceive as pure wizardry.

Python's core philosophy is summarized in The Zen of Python, and it paints the colorful rules that govern the language as:

1. Explicit is better than implicit
2. Simply is better than complex
3. Complexly is better than complicated
4. Beautifully is better than ugly
5. Readability counts

As a testament to just how beautiful Python code can be, this is how exercise 37 looks on my editor:

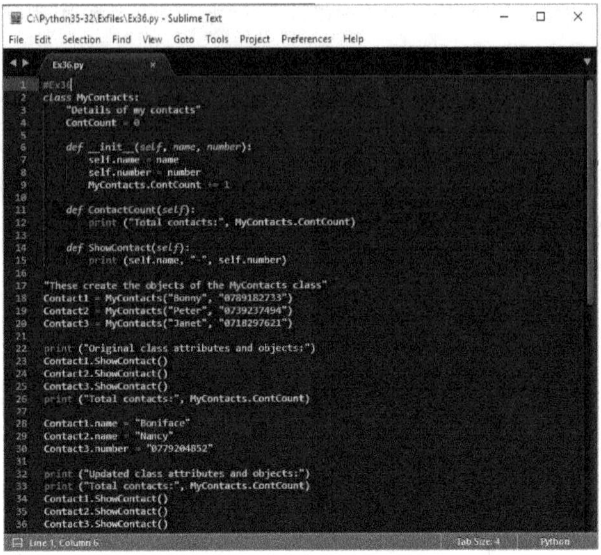

C:\Python35-32\Exfiles\Ex36.py - Sublime Text

File Edit Selection Find View Goto Tools Project Preferences Help

Ex36.py

```
#Ex36
class MyContacts:
    "Details of my contacts"
    ContCount = 0

    def __init__(self, name, number):
        self.name = name
        self.number = number
        MyContacts.ContCount += 1

    def ContactCount(self):
        print ("Total contacts:", MyContacts.ContCount)

    def ShowContact(self):
        print (self.name, "-", self.number)

"These create the objects of the MyContacts class"
Contact1 = MyContacts("Bonny", "0789182733")
Contact2 = MyContacts("Peter", "0739237494")
Contact3 = MyContacts("Janet", "0718297621")

print ("Original class attributes and objects:")
Contact1.ShowContact()
Contact2.ShowContact()
Contact3.ShowContact()
print ("Total contacts:", MyContacts.ContCount)

Contact1.name = "Boniface"
Contact2.name = "Nancy"
Contact3.number = "0779204852"

print ("Updated class attributes and objects:")
print ("Total contacts:", MyContacts.ContCount)
Contact1.ShowContact()
Contact2.ShowContact()
Contact3.ShowContact()
```

Line 1, Column 6 Tab Size: 4 Python

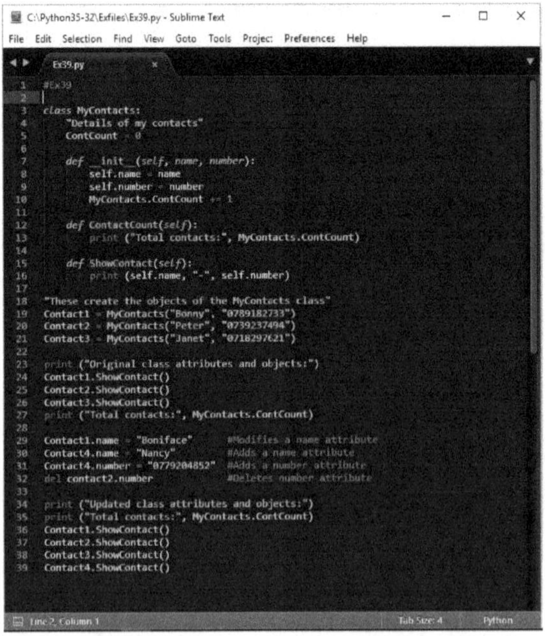

C:\Python35-32\Exfiles\Ex39.py - Sublime Text

File Edit Selection Find View Goto Tools Project Preferences Help

Ex39.py

```
#Ex39

class MyContacts:
    "Details of my contacts"
    ContCount = 0

    def __init__(self, name, number):
        self.name = name
        self.number = number
        MyContacts.ContCount += 1

    def ContactCount(self):
        print ("Total contacts:", MyContacts.ContCount)

    def ShowContact(self):
        print (self.name, "-", self.number)

"These create the objects of the MyContacts class"
Contact1 = MyContacts("Bonny", "0789182733")
Contact2 = MyContacts("Peter", "0739237494")
Contact3 = MyContacts("Janet", "0718297621")

print ("Original class attributes and objects:")
Contact1.ShowContact()
Contact2.ShowContact()
Contact3.ShowContact()
print ("Total contacts:", MyContacts.ContCount)

Contact1.name = "Boniface"      #Modifies a name attribute
Contact4.name = "Nancy"         #Adds a name attribute
Contact4.number = "0779204852"  #Adds a number attribute
del contact2.number             #Deletes number attribute

print ("Updated class attributes and objects:")
print ("Total contacts:", MyContacts.ContCount)
Contact1.ShowContact()
Contact2.ShowContact()
Contact3.ShowContact()
Contact4.ShowContact()
```

Line 2, Column 1 Tab Size: 4 Python

It is more important now more than ever that you re-visit everything you learned from Hour 1 and practice every day and create much more scripts that do many different things. The internet is full of resources including challenges to create Python scripts that solve all kinds of problems that you can learn from.

You have come this far, and it shows how much passion you have in becoming better at programming, toast yourself but strive to save 100 .py scripts with tens, maybe hundreds of lines of beautiful code over the next week of study. Explore what the world of Python has to offer and be an active member of Github and a StackOverflow.

There are multitudinous ways you can practice and advance your coding skills every day. Every day, thousands of programmers meet on CodeFights and head writing Python code. It has become a large community of upcoming programmers who have turned learning to create solutions to problems we face everyday pillow fights. You can have fun there, or perhaps in the future, you will take a more ambitious approach and get a certification in Python programming from edX and turn it into a career.

Don't forget to get the FREE "Cyberpunk Python Whizz Kit" if you haven't already. This will help you tremendously in getting the most out of this book.

Links

Here are a parting gift and a pointer to the right direction: A list of the most useful resources you should consider checking out. Write a program to save this list and use it every day to find answers you might have about your code. Perhaps someday you will` be writing programs for your home devices including the TV and lighting system or you might push the envelope and create apps for your own AI running on a $35 Raspberry Pi computer.

Good luck.

Tools

1. Python.org.

This is the official website with all the technical details about the Python programming language.

2. Using Algorithms and Data Structures in Python

http://interactivepython.org/runestone/static/pythonds/index.html

3. Python visualizer tool

http://people.csail.mit.edu/pgbovine/python/tutor.html

4. Thonny, Python IDE for beginners.

This one has intuitive features useful for program runtime visualization

http://thonny.org/

5. Python Essential Reference

http://www.worldcat.org/title/python-essential-reference/oclc/288985690

Course

1. Google's Python class

https://code.google.com/edu/languages/google-python-class/

2. MIT's Using Python for Research

https://www.edx.org/course/using-python-research-harvardx-ph526x

3. 6.00.1x: Introduction to Computer Science and Programming Using Python

http://ocw.mit.edu/courses/electrical-engineering-and-computer-science/6-00-introduction-to-computer-science-and-programming-fall-2008/

https://www.edx.org/course/introduction-computer-science-mitx-6-00-1x-9

https://www.class-central.com/mooc/1341/edx-6-00-1x-introduction-to-computer-science-and-programming-using-python

4. uDemy's Learn Python (for Beginners)

Online course

http://www.udemy.com/learning-python-not-the-snake/

Websites and Tutorials

10. Checking interactive learning resource

A creative way to boost your Python skills through interesting tasks.

http://www.checkio.org/

11. Interactive tutorials on Python

This tutorial for beginners has beautiful interactive examples.

http://jwork.org/learn/doc/doku.php?id=python:start

12. ComparingTypes

Learn how Python relates and compares with other languages. How it is similar with its sister Perl, cousin Java, and an overview of how it was a BIG improvement from ABC.

https://wiki.python.org/moin/ComparingTypes

13. Python Programming Tutorials

More Python tutorials.

https://pythonspot.com/

http://thepythonguru.com/getting-started-with-python/

Interactive Tools and Lessons

14. LearnStreet

A free online Python tutorial with practice exercises

http://www.learnstreet.com/

15. Interactive tutorials for scientific programming using Python

Python tutorials in the video.

http://jwork.org/learn/

16. ShowMeDo

http://showmedo.com/videos/python

Over 240 screencasts that reveal the best secrets about Python as the language of the future.

17. Python Bits

A YouTube playlist is covering interesting Python topics. Ideal for beginners and intermediate learners.

https://www.youtube.com/c/ArtheadSe

18. Envato Tuts+

More Python video tutorials

https://code.tutsplus.com/

19. CodeFights

Compete with bots and humans writing problem-solving programs and mastering Python – in real-time.

https://codefights.com/

Raspberry Pi:

The No-Nonsense

Guide

Learn How To Program Your Raspberry Pi 3 Within 12 Hours!

CYBERPUNK UNIVERSITY

Disclaimer Notice:

Table of Contents

Introduction 1

Hour 1: Getting Started with the Raspberry Pi 3

1.1 About Raspberry Foundation 3

1.2 What is Raspberry Pi? 4

1.3 Technical specs of the Raspberry Pi board 5

1.4 Defining the GPIO 6

1.5 For what do you need this book? 6

Hour 2: Setting Up the Raspberry Pi 10

2.1 Raspbian OS for your Raspberry Pi 10

2.2 Downloading and Installing Raspbian OS 11

Step 1: Get everything ready 11

Step 2: Write Image to disk 12

Step 3: Assemble the Raspberry Pi 12

Step 4: Install Raspbian OS 12

Step 5: Configure Wi-Fi or LAN network 13

Step 6: Connect Bluetooth Devices 13

Hour 3: Installing Raspbian OS the Hard Way 15

3.1 Is the hard way the better way? 15

Step 1: Get everything ready 16

Step 2: Writing image to disk 17

Step 3: Installing Raspbian OS on the Pi 17

Step 4: Reboot 19

3.6 Understanding the raspi-config window 20

Hour 4: The Basics about Raspbian OS 22

4.1 Connecting to a network 22

4.2 Using Raspbian on Raspberry Pi as a desktop PC 23

4.3 Exploring apps and packages 24

4.4 Updating Software 24

4.5 Installing new software 25

Hour 5: Writing a Simple Game with Scratch on Raspberry Pi 28

5.1 What is scratch? 28

5.2 Variables 30

5.3 Blocks 31

5.4 Creating a simple arcade game based on the popular Ping pong 31

Step 1: Setting up Scratch 32

Step 2: Making the ball bouncy 34

Step 3: The ball and the bat 36

Step 4: Configuring player control 38

Step 5: Program the opponentbat to play intelligently 39

Step 6: Variables and keeping score 40

5.5 Conclusion 42

Hour 6: The GPIO (General Purpose Input and Output) 43

6.1 Understanding the GPIO on Raspberry Pi 43

Hour 7: Making an LED Blink with Scratch GPIO on Raspberry Pi 46

7.1 Getting everything ready 46

7.2 Usage and basic capabilities of GPIO server 47

7.3 Connecting the hardware 48

7.4 Configuring GPIO pins on Scratch 49

7.5 Conclusion 52

Hour 8: Introduction to the Shell on Raspberry Pi 53

8.1 What is the Shell or Terminal 53
8.2 Discovering basic commands in Unix 54
8.3 Summary 57
Hour 9: Programming the Raspberry Pi with Python 58
9.1 What is Python? 58
9.2 Hello World! on Raspberry Pi 59
9.3 Running a saved Python file 62
9.4 Learning to program Python 63
9.5 Conclusion 63
Hour 10: Writing More Code for Raspberry Pi in Python 65
10.1 Input programming with Python 65
10.2 Adding comments to a Python script 67
10.3 Output programming in a Python script 68
10.4 Programming the GPIO with simple code 69
10.5 Making the LED light blink 70
Hour 11: Reading and writing from GPIO ports from Python 74
11.1 Switching an LED on and off 74
11.2 Connecting a push button to get input 76
11.3 Controlling an LED bulb with a push button using Python 78
11.4 Controlling the Brightness of an LED 79
11.5 Programming a button that toggles an LED on or off 80
Hour 12: How to Get the Most out of your Raspberry Pi 82
12.1 Try different operating systems 82
12.2 Get a case with a built-in heat sink 84
12.3 Explore a world of amazing learner projects 74

BONUS #1: Raspberry Pi 3 Pinout Chart 86

BONUS #2: The Top 6 Raspberry Pi Projects for Beginners 87

1. DIY Raspberry Pi Music Player 87
2. Raspberry Pi Twitterbot 88
3. Raspberry Pi Personal Assistant. 89
4. Raspberry Pi Weather Station 90
5. Raspberry Pi Wall Mounted Google Calendar 91
6. Raspberry Pi Personal Cloud Storage 92

Introduction

You saw the cool project Raspberry Pi owners share online; read an article or two about how there is a $35 card-sized computer that you can program to do magical things; You probably even discovered that you always wished you could learn Python programming language; All these conspired to convince you to buy the Raspberry Pi. Now you have it, what's next?

Buying this guide is the best decision you have made as a first-time Raspberry Pi owner. This is a simplified guide that introduces the basics about the Pi including how to connect and configure it, how to write computer programs for it used on-board tools just by drag-and-drop, and how to write your first Python code that controls a blinking LED.

Yes, this is an introductory guide to Raspberry Pi 3, but it goes in a lot deeper than just tell you what it is. With simple step-by-step instructions you will find easy to follow, this book is the best resource to understand how to make your Pi solve your problems. Isn't that why we have computers in the first place?

This eBook is structured into 12 practical chapters that take roughly an hour to do. We have designed the content of the book to be easy to follow for both complete beginners to programming and those with knowledge of other programming languages as well as beginners to Linux and Linux gurus.

Cyberpunk University is committed to producing content that helps learners discover their coding skills and to learn processes that make it easy for them to think of solutions to daily human problems. Many other programming and DIY books are coming in the future so be sure to check our catalog and get the chance to learn even more ways to write programs in different languages that computers can understand.

Find out more about our other books in the series:

1. Python: The No-Nonsense Guide, Learn Python Programming Within 12 Hours!

2. Hacking: The No-Nonsense Guide, Learn Ethical Hacking Within 12 Hours!

Hour 1: Getting Started with the Raspberry Pi

1.1 About Raspberry Foundation

The Raspberry Pi Foundation is a non-profit organization that came up with the ingenious idea to make a full computer the size of a credit card, originally intended for learners in the developing world. The organization released the third edition of its bestselling device in 2015 aptly dubbed Raspberry Pi 3. The tiny machine with a load of capabilities is described as a full desktop PC that can be programmed to do almost anything from creating home servers and media centers to controlling game consoles and document processing.

The Raspberry Pi 3 or simply Pi3 features a 64-bit 1.2 GHz quad-core ARM Cortex A53 processor and comes with Wi-Fi, Bluetooth, Ethernet, and USB on board. Enthusiasts all over the world are constantly posting details of the amazing things they have managed to turn the Pi into, including responsive mirrors, tor routers, video surveillance centers, and even virtual computers for windows operating systems.

Now that you are introduced to Raspberry Pi 3 and possibly already have one on your experimentation bench, you are on the verge of doing amazing things with it using just simple code. You do not need to be a programmer to create dazzling projects with the Pi, but you must be willing and open to learn and try new things.

There is a lot to discover in the Raspberry Pi. If you have already ordered one, then you are in the right path to learning and putting into practice a world of applications of such a tiny yet powerful computer.

In this first hour of discovering the 12 hour guide for programming the Raspberry Pi, we will delve into what it is, a bit of its history, and anything else important you need to know about this compact system.

1.2 What is Raspberry Pi?

The Raspberry Pi Foundation was founded in 2012 to make computers and computer programming instructions accessible to everyone for cheap. While the original mission of the organization was to develop inexpensive computers ready for programming and avail them to students, a much diverse audience has embraced the Pi.

Professional programmers, tinkers, DIYers, and curious hobbyist have embraced the tiny machine and as a result, the support community for the device has grown tremendously around the world in just over five years.

The original Raspberry Pi (called Pi 1 model A) had a SoC (System on Chip) setup built around the tiny but powerful Broadcom BCM 2835 processor commonly used in cellphones. The system included a processor, GPU, and audio and video processing among other features on the low-power chip.

The latest installment, the Pi 3, is even more powerful with greater capabilities including Bluetooth 4.0, Wi-Fi, and a quad-core processing within the same board size as Pi 1. The Pi 3 is a versatile computer that can run many distributions of Linux (including those with desktop environments). However, there are stripped down versions of the open source operating system built specifically for it as you will discover in a bit.

1.3 Technical specs of the Raspberry Pi board

If you are a hardware aficionado, you will be impressed by how much power the credit card-sized Pi computer packs. In the early years of the Pi foundation, two versions of the Raspberry Pi were released. Model A that cost $25 and Model B that cost $35. Model A had no Ethernet port, one less USB port, and half the RAM of its brother Model B.

As the Pi gained more attention and publicity, it was able to pump up the hardware specs significantly while maintaining the price of the Model B, which they decided to focus on. There was only one version of Raspberry Pi 2 and now 3.

So, what exactly do you get when you fork out $35 for Raspberry Pi 3? This:

Raspberry Pi 3 board.

- ✧ GHz ARM System on Chip (SOC) processor with integrated 1 GB RAM.
- ✧ 1 HDMI port for digital video and audio output.
- ✧ 3.5 mm for composite video and analogue output.

- ✧ 4 USB 2.0 ports.
- ✧ 1 microSD memory card reader.
- ✧ 1 Ethernet LAN port.
- ✧ 1 integrated Wi-Fi and Bluetooth radio antenna.
- ✧ 1 MicroUSB power port.
- ✧ GPIO (General Purpose Input/Output) interface.

1.4 Defining the GPIO

The General Purpose Input and Output interface is a set of 40 vertical exposed pins on the Raspberry Pi that are not linked to any specific native functions on the board. These pins are put in place so that the end user can have a low-level access directly to the hardware. He can attach other hardware boards, LCD and LED screens, peripheral devices, and many other kinds of hardware.

As you learn how to program the Pi, you will discover just how ingenious it is that the designers chose to include such an authentic interface for the hardware you will be attaching your own and third party hardware.

1.5 For what do you need this book?

When you order the Raspberry Pi 3, you will get just the bare board -- no case, cables, or power connectors and no guide. Just the board. This means you will have to purchase all the connectors and accessories you will need separately and rely on people like us to learn how to build stuff. Here is a list of the most important things you will need to get (if you don't already have them lying around your workshop).

1. This simplified guide book

2. A stable power source

The Raspberry Pi gets its power via a microUSB port. This means you will need a standard AC to microUSB adapter that can provide consistent 5v power output at a minimum 700mA.

2. A 4GB microSD memory card

The Raspberry Pi foundation recommends that you have a microSD card with at least 4GB available space to install the operating system and applications on the Pi. However, an 8GB or larger card would be ideal. Memory cards are very cheap today, you should consider getting at least a 16GB Class 10 microSD card or larger so that you will never have to worry about storage space.

3. Audio/Visual cables:

What video output do you intend to connect your Pi? If you have a HDTV or one of those newer computer monitors or TVs with HDMI support, you should buy an HDMI cable for digital video and audio output. If your have a standard computer monitor without HDMI support, you will need an HDMI to DVi converter cable for video and a 3.5mm cable for analog audio.

For connection to older TVs, you can buy an RCA cable for video and the 3.5mm stereo cable for audio. If you are unsure which cable is which, head on to the Raspberry Pi website and read official recommendations before you purchase one.

HDMI connector HDMI to DVI lead RCA composite video connector

4. Ethernet cable and Router

Although it is not an absolute necessity, connecting the Pi to a network is important, especially for downloading and updating software. It makes everything so easy and fast. An Ethernet cable that connects to a router is necessary if your project relies on you being connected to the internet via LAN.

The Pi comes with an Ethernet port on board, so you will just need to get a cable to plug it to the router. If you would rather use Wi-Fi, the Pi also has that built-in.

5. Mouse and Keyboard:

No matter what you intend to use your Pi for, you will still need a mouse and keyboard to set it up and get it running. Any standard USB keyboard and mouse should work without a problem. These input devices will draw power from the board's USB ports, but a negligible 100mAh or so each. You can check out eLinux.org for a list of verified peripherals compatible with the Raspberry Pi.

Optional: A case:

The Raspberry Pi ships naked. You will get a naked board. For a very small price, though, you can buy a proper case and enclose it to give it a more 'computer' feel and to protect it from the elements and accidental damage. An acrylic or plastic case costs less than $10 but you can also build your own case. Before you purchase one, be sure that you are buying a case for the right Pi because cases for older models will not fit the Pi 3 snugly.

Different Raspberry Pi 3 casings

NOTE: Raspberry Pi Foundation, as I have mentioned earlier, is a non-profit organization. This is why they can afford to sell us such a great computer at a ridiculously low price. The organization runs on support from people like us – through donations and lately by selling official casings of the Raspberry Pi. If you are considering buying a case for your hardware, you should buy one from the foundation and not third-party manufacturers and offer your support a worthy cause.

Hour 2: Setting Up the Raspberry Pi

The Raspberry Pi does not come with an operating system, you have to download and set it up yourself. This, however, is not a weakness but a feature. It means you get to choose from a wide variety of operating systems available to find one that meets your needs.

NOOBS, acronym for New Out Of the Box Software is a program that manages and installs the operating system on your device. This will make it easy for you to install the OS of your choice and to set up the Raspberry Pi.

2.1 Raspbian OS for your Raspberry Pi

There is a wide range of operating systems to choose from for the Pi, all of which are available online for download. Some of the most popular operating systems out there today are Raspbian (Linux distro specially built for the Pi), XBMC, OSMC, RISC OS, OpenELEC, ArchLinux, and Windows IoT Core among others. We have introduced a few of these in Hour 12 of the book.

Raspbian is by far the best and all-round operating system for the Pi. It is also considered the “official” system that every beginner should start with. It is a version of Linux modified for for the Pi and it is what we will be setting up and running in this book. It is packed with all the essential software you need for almost every basic computer task including document processing, browsing the web, checking your emails, and even programming in Python.

If you are new to Linux, you may find Raspbian a bit confusing but do not worry; there are great resources online that will help you navigate this new ocean and explore endless possibilities. A great place to start is the Official Raspberry Pi Beginners Wiki on eLinux.org. They also have a great YouTube channel that explains everything you will need to know to become a master-Raspbian.

2.2 Downloading and Installing Raspbian OS

NOOBS is a great way to test out your new OS and get to know the workings of Raspberry Pi. It makes the OS easy to install right on the memory card. If you would rather not handle the technical aspects of writing an image file to disk, you can grab a pre-installed memory card from Adafruit for about $12. You will find a full guide video on how to work with NOOBS on the Raspberry Pi help page.

Step 1: Get everything ready

NOOBS streamlines the installation process for your Raspbian OS. Get everything you need ready by first downloading NOOBS from this RaspberryPi.org. There are two versions of the download: A larger file for offline and network install, which comes with Raspbian OS in it and a smaller file for online install. I suggest that you download the offline installer and save it on your computer.

You will also need an application to format your SD memory card before you transfer the software on to it. For this, you can download the SD Formatter app from the SD Association. There is a version for both Windows and Mac OS X. Use this tool to format your memory card and prepare it for copying files.

Step 2: Write Image to disk

Once your SD card formatting is complete, extract the zipped files to a folder then transfer all files on to the root of the memory card. These files will include NOOBS and Raspbian OS files.

Wait for the process to complete then eject the memory card.

Step 3: Assemble the Raspberry Pi

Connecting peripheral devices to your Raspberry Pi may be the easiest thing you can do at this stage, but it is important to know what order to follow so that it can recognize all the devices when it boots up.

First, connect the HDMI or monitor cable then connect the USB mouse and keyboard. If you intend to connect the Pi to a LAN network via a router, connect the Ethernet cable next. Finally, insert the memory card with your copied NOOBS and Raspbian OS files.

Because Raspberry Pi does not have a power switch, it powers on the moment you connect and turn on the power. Connect the power USB cable last then switch power on. Your newest computer will boot to the NOOBS screen which will allow you to set up the OS.

Step 4: Install Raspbian OS

The NOOBS system will take a couple of minutes to get all the devices ready. Let it do its thing, eventually it will complete the checks and take you to a screen prompting you to install an operating system.

At the bottom of this screen, you will see the options to choose your language and keyboard layout. Make your selections then click the check box next to the Raspbian option and click install to initiate the process.

That is it! NOOBS will take over and run the installation process, which could take anywhere between ten and twenty minutes. When the setup is complete, NOOBS will restart the Pi and it will boot right to the new Linux Raspbian OS desktop where you can begin configuring everything else.

Note: Should the installation process require a username and password, the defaults to use are:

Username: pi

Password: raspberry

Step 5: Configure Wi-Fi or LAN network

The Raspbian OS has a very intuitive screen featuring a 'start' Pi menu where you can start applications and tools, open the file browser or go online—pretty much everything you would expect on a full-fledged desktop environment. First though, you should set up a network connection.

To connect to a Wi-Fi network, click on the network icon on the top right corner. It is the icon with two computers.

Select your Wi-Fi network by clicking on its SSID. This will prompt you to enter a password. Enter the wireless network password then click OK to connect.

The process is the same when you are connecting to Ethernet wired network.

Step 6: Connect Bluetooth Devices

If you have Bluetooth devices such as a keyboard and mouse or speakers, you will need to pair them with the Raspberry Pi before you can use them. This, however, depends on the devices and your pairing preferences.

The process is pretty straightforward on Raspbian. Simply click the Bluetooth icon on the top right corner of the screen and select 'Add Device'. The system will scan for discoverable Bluetooth devices and when it finds the device you want to pair, simply click on it and click pair. A simplified pairing process will guide you on what to do until the process is completed.

That is it as far as setting up and configuring your Pi goes! As you can see, the process has been simplified by NOOBS. Setting up Raspberry Pi 1 and 2 was such a pain, but thanks to the NOOBS program, anyone can now get the Pi running without writing cryptic lines of code. If anything should go wrong during the setup process, just start over more carefully and follow the above process to re-install Raspbian.

Hour 3: Installing Raspbian OS the Hard Way

Installing an operating system on a Raspberry Pi is too easy with NOOBS, which makes sense because that is what NOOBS was developed for. Unfortunately, the process explained in the last hour does not go deep to show exactly what is happening during the installation process. If you are the kind of person who likes to do things the hard way, in this hour that is exactly what we are going to focus on.

3.1 Is the hard way the better way?

One of the biggest problem that beginners face when trying to install Raspbian or any other OS for that matter on Raspberry Pi is low space. If you have a 4GB microSD card, you will fit the NOOBS files on it, but there may not be sufficient space to carry out the installation because it involves expanding files, not to mention space for your files after the installation is complete.

Besides, if you have gone as far as buy your own Pi, it would be understandable that you want to use the more technical approach to installing the OS. As you begin programming the Pi, it will pay off having a clear understanding of how the system works and how to set it up without taking shortcuts.

Also, considering that this book does not dive deep into the various ways to test an OS before installing it on your Pi, it will be important to know how to perform the setup process using the terminal for when you install another operating system or to repair the current one.

In this hour, we will look at how to install Raspbian OS on your Pi using the not-too-easy approach. Let's start.

Step 1: Get everything ready

Head over to the Raspberry Pi Downloads page and download the latest Raspbian OS image. There are two versions of the Raspbian OS image: a pixel image Raspbian Jessie, and the Raspbian Jessie Lite, a minimal version of the OS that is smaller in size. Decide which one you wish to install then download it.

You will also need a tool to extract the file image from the archive. You can use 7Zip for windows or Unarchiver for Mac. Both these tools are available free online.

As with the previous method, you will need a tool to format your memory card. Use the SD Formatter from SDcard.org you downloaded in the previous hour. Finally, you will need a tool to write the downloaded OS files you extract from the archive on to the memory card. You can download the Win32 Disk Imager for that. You can download it from Sourceforge.

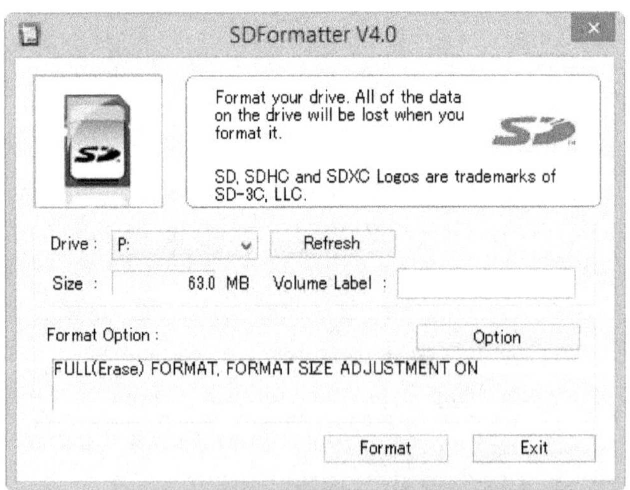

MicroSD Formatting app SDFormatter

Step 2: Writing image to disk

Begin the installation by formatting the disk. You can begin the process and let it run in the background. Meanwhile, extract the .img file of the OS image in the archive you downloaded and place it on a folder where you can easily access.

Run the Win32 Disk Imager with administrative rights on Windows. Select the Raspbian OS .img file you extracted and load it. When the SD card formatting is complete, select the disk address as the destination on the Win32 Disk Imager then click Write to begin the process.

Writing to the disk may take up to 30 minutes. Be patient till it is done then remove the SD card.

Step 3: Installing Raspbian OS on the Pi

This is the step where the excitement begins. As explained in the previous hour, the order in which you connect your devices to the Pi matters. It is recommended that you do not power on the device before you connect the keyboard and mouse.

Insert the memory card and plug in the mouse and keyboard then connect the power cable. The Pi should power on and start booting after you turn the power on.

If you are prompted to enter your credentials the defaults are:

Login: pi

Password: raspberry

When boot up is complete, you will be taken to the configuration screen titled 'Setup Options'. This is how it should look like:

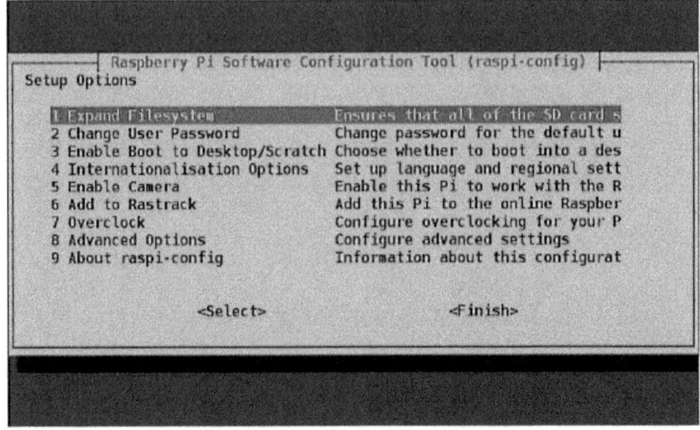

If you do not see the setup options screen you can get to it by starting the terminal then entering the following command:

sudo raspi-config

Select the first option:

1 Expand Filesystem

Do this by pressing the return key on the keyboard (Enter). Setup will use up all the space in the SD card as a single partition to install the operating system. It does this by expanding the Raspian OS image to fit the available storage space.

When this is done, you will return to the same screen where you can then select the third option:

3 Enable Boot to Desktop/Scratch

In the next screen, you will be asked to 'Choose boot option'. Select the second option:

Desktop Log in as user 'pi' at the graphical desktop

Click OK or press enter. We select this option so that when the Raspbian boots up, each time it will take us to the graphical user interface desktop and not the Terminal.

When this is done, the raspi-config will take you back to the previous window, the Setup Options page.

Step 4: Reboot

In some cases, the Pi may automatically reboot after the setup is done. If it does not, you may have to boot it manually. You can do this on the Terminal using the command:

```
sudo reboot
```

If everything went right during the setup, the Pi should boot to a beautiful graphical user interface desktop. You are now ready to start doing magic with your Pi.

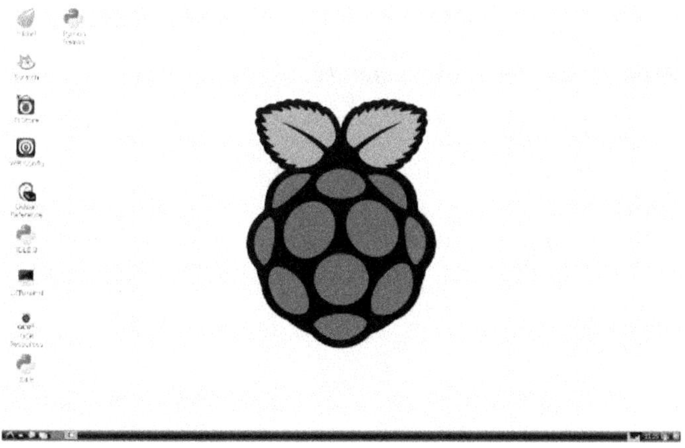

Raspbian OS desktop on Raspberry Pi 3

3.6 Understanding the raspi-config window

The Raspberry Pi configuration window, powered by raspi-config engine, has more options than we used in the setup process above. As you begin to understand how your device works, it is good for you to know what each of the nine items on the Setup Options window does for when you will need to use it. All of them have a brief explanation about what they do to their right but here is a summary that may be easier to understand:

1. Expand Filesystem: As mentioned, this option expands the operating system image to occupy the entire disk. You do not need to expand the image but it is highly recommended that you do so to make use of all the storage space available.

Any unused space on the SD card may not be recognized by the Pi, which means it will go to waste and you will have lesser disk space for your projects.

2. Change User Password: This is pretty straightforward. You can choose change the default password from raspberry on this screen.

3. Enable Boot to Desktop/Scratch: This option allows you to change where your Pi boots to. You can choose to boot straight to Scratch, to the Terminal, or to the gui desktop.

4. Internationalisation Options: Here you can set or change your locale, timezone, and keyboard layout. Note that you will need to reboot the Pi to apply your changes.

5. Enable Camera: Enable this to use the Raspberry Pi Camera Module. When enabled, the system will dedicate at least 128MB of RAM to the GPU.

6. Add to Rastrack: This is a handy feature if you want to know who else around you uses the Pi. It is user-contributed and runs on Google's Maps to allow users to add their locations. Rastrack shows a heat map of where Pi users are around the world.

7. Overclock: The default clock speed of the Pi's processor is 700MHz but you can pump it up to 1000MHz with this option. Note that the results you achieve may vary and that overclocking too high could cause instability that reduces the life of your Pi.

8. Advanced options: There are several important options under this item, some of which we will look at in the next steps we will cover in the book. They are:

Overscan	Hostname	Memory Split	SSH	Device tree
SPI	I2C	Serial	Audio	Update

9. About raspi-config: A two-sentence summary of what the Pi is all about.

Hour 4: The Basics about Raspbian OS

Learning how to work with and program your Raspberry Pi is much easier and faster when you start somewhere familiar. Where could be better than a dynamic graphical user interface of Raspbian OS?

Raspbian was developed with a goal to become the top OS of choice for all kinds of Pi users – from beginners like you to the veterans who pride themselves in having owned the very first Raspberry Pi model A back in 2012.

Raspbian was developed based on the Debian distribution of Linux, hence the reason they are very similar in many ways. Debian has millions of users around the world who have contributed a massive knowledge base and documentation published on the web. Raspbian users can tap on this wealth of information to learn broadly and deeply about Raspbian OS. Almost every piece of information about Debian OS you find on the web also applies to Raspbian OS of the same version on the Pi.

4.1 Connecting to a network

One of the very first things that Pi users do as soon as they have set up their devices is to connect to the internet – either by setting up the LAN or by connecting to Wi-Fi. The setup process is pretty simple.

If connecting to a router via an Ethernet cable, you need to configure your routers DHCP so that you can easily plug in the cable and connect to it. If you already have a router and a network, we will assume you have already figured out its settings and how to add a new computer to the network.

For Wi-Fi connections, it is even easier to set up the Pi to join the network and connect to the internet. Raspbian comes with a handy Wi-Fi Config tool, whose shortcut is placed on the desktop. All you just need to double-click and follow simple guided steps to connect to the hotspot or Wi-Fi network.

If you have to scan for networks, you can use the following commands on the LXTerminal:

```
sudo iwlist wlan0 scan
```

This command will scan and list all the available networks for you to choose the one you want to connect to.

To connect to the network manually, open the nano editor and modify the configuration file wpa-supplicant using the following command:

```
sudo nano /etc/wpa_supplicant/wpa_supplicant.conf
```

Scroll to the bottom of the file and enter the network information in this format:

```
network = {
    ssid = "[Wi-Fi_ESSID]"
    psk = "[Wi-Fi_password]"
    }
```

Save the file and the wpa-supplicant will begin to connect to the network in a few seconds.

4.2 Using Raspbian on Raspberry Pi as a desktop PC

The most important part of setting up your Raspberry Pi is installing the operating system. Once you are done with this step, and the OS of your choice is running seamlessly, you can decide to turn your Pi into anything you want – from a desktop PC or server to a bot or a game console.

Since we have installed the most basic (and most suited) operating system on the Pi, we will first look at what you need to do to turn it into a potent PC that you can use for anything that your Windows, Linux, or Mac desktop computer does.

Considering that Raspbian OS is based on Linux kernel, the following steps will be much easier for you if you are familiar with the Linux platform in general. Do not worry though, you will still find it easy to learn if this is your first encounter with the Linux operating system. This guide is written for you.

4.3 Exploring apps and packages

If you have already explored around the desktop of the Raspbian OS, you may have noticed that it comes pre-installed with several tools you would need for a basic PC. As long as your display is good, you can easily navigate to any apps (called packages) or settings installed by double-clicking the icon shortcuts on the desktop and via the 'Start' button on the top left corner of the screen.

Under the office header, you find the entire suite of word processor, spreadsheet, presentation, database, etc. You will also find shortcuts on the desktop to popular tools and packages you will be using including Python IDLE and games.

There is an even easier way to explore hundreds of other packages and download them with ease: the Raspbian store also dubbed The Pi Store. You can add the Pi Store app to your installation using the command:

```
sudo apt-get update && sudo apt-get install pistore
```

4.4 Updating Software

The first thing you should do is upgrade the system's package list.

Open the LXTerminal by double-clicking the shortcut on the desktop or press Ctrl+Alt+T on your keyboard. Then enter this code to update the package list:

```
sudo apt-get update
```

You may be asked to enter root password. The default root username is 'root' and the password is 'root'.

Next, upgrade the packages already installed using the following command:

```
sudo apt-get dist-upgrade
```

This command enables the APT (Advanced Packaging Tool) to update your packages regularly. It will also download and install any new kernel and firmware updates of the Debian package. Note, however, that these packages are not frequently updated; updates are only rolled out after extensive testing.

4.5 Installing new software

There is a very simple way to install software on your Pi than having to go online on a browser, download a package, unzip it, and begin configuration: The APT tool.

This tool allows you to install, update, and uninstall packages with a simple command. If a software program is packaged for Debian and it is developed to work on the Pi's ARM architecture, then you should be able to install it using the apt-get command.

As you have noticed above, you will need to gain root access using the sudo command to use apt-get. The command sudo stands for Super User DO and it essentially grants the installation tool superuser (system-level) privileges to configure the packages. This is the reason you have to enter a password to be logged in as root or a sudoer.

To see a list of software sources that APT keeps, you can open the sources.list file stored in the directory /etc/apt/. You will find out as you get more experience why this is important.

The command to install a package takes this format:

```
sudo apt-get install package_name
```

The update procedure we covered in the previous section updates all the packages including firmware. If you have limited bandwidth or disk space and wish to update only a specific package at a time, you can use this command:

```
sudo apt-get update package_name
```

Here is the apt command you will use to uninstall a package:

```
sudo apt-get remove package_name
```

This will prompt you to confirm the uninstallation with a y/n question. However, if you do not want to be constantly asked to confirm, you can use the –y flag after the package_name to auto confirm.

An alternative command to remove a program is purge. The purge APT command removes the package and all its associated configuration files. The command looks like this:

```
sudo apt-get purge package_name
```

It is advisable that you do not use purge unless you know what you are doing.

If you have the name of a package you wish to install, you can search for it using the command:

```
apt-cache search package_name
```

Finally, the tree command may come in handy, especially if you want to get even more familiar with the terminal interface. This command visualizes the structure of your working directory (called present working directory or pwd). Type the command and see how it works.

```
tree
```

Hour 5: Writing a Simple Game with Scratch on Raspberry Pi

Now that we have covered all the basics about the Raspberry Pi, our next step is to learn how to use it to make things happen. In this hour, we are going to learn how to develop a simple game using a bundled tool whose shortcut you will find on the desktop: Scratch.

This hour, you will learn to get around the interface of scratch, practice using blocks to program an object to move, change sprites, and even create your own sprites.

Fig 1: Scratch on Raspberry Pi

5.1 What is scratch?

Scratch is a visual programming tool that comes with the Raspbian OS. It allows you to create games and animations with ease using a drag-and-drop interface. This tool makes programming easy, and fun—even addicting. You can also use an online browser version of this tool.

With scratch, we will be able to create a simple game with guidance on this book, but later you can practice on your own to create interactive stories, animations, and even use it to program the GPIO pins on the Pi. This tool is the best introduction to code and especially game programming because you will not need to write the actual code. It will help you understand the general aspects and techniques of programming that will lay the foundation for your understanding of the more complex procedures later on.

Scratch is already installed on your Pi, you will not need to download or install anything. Simply open the package from the desktop icon and you are good to go. The main window of the app is split into three sections:

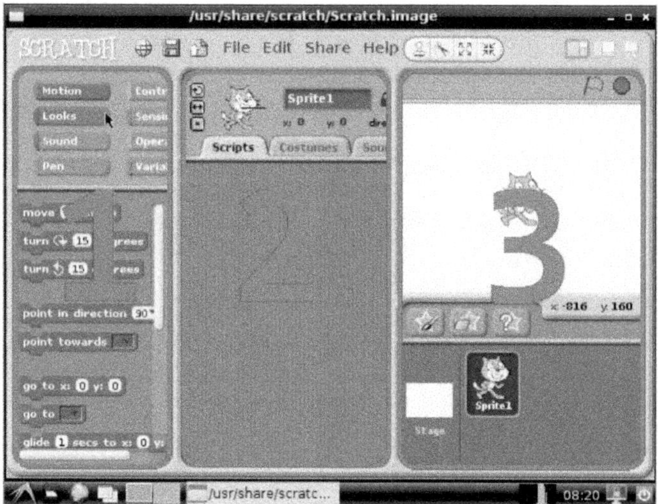

1. The tools you will need to create your game are on the left.
2. The middle section is your working area where you will create the sprites and steps.
3. The program you create will run on the right section.

Your game will be made up of sprites (pictures) that follow scripts (steps) you create. The scripts are what we use to control what the program does when a certain condition is met, such as when the player presses a key.

On the top left corner, you will see eight buttons (tools). They are: Motion, Looks, Sound, Pen, Control, Sensing, Operations, and Variables. These are the categories of the pieces we will be dragging and adding on to the scripts to build our game.

Let's get started.

5.2 Variables

Before we can begin creating our game on Scratch, there are a few things we must understand. First, is that the program should able to remember something. Could be a shape, a number, an event, text—anything. We will do this using variables.

A variable is a small allocation of computer memory that a program stores data in. We will create several variables during the game to store game data. If you have learnt other languages of programming, such as Python, you will discover that there are different types of variables, each specific to storing a particular type of data. In this section, however, you do not need to worry about all that.

CyberPunk University has a comprehensive yet simplified eBook that can help you understand full computer programming 'Python: The No-Nonsense Guide'. Sooner or later, if you find programming with the Raspberry Pi fun and productive, you will need a full guide such as this to learn everything.

Every variable we will create will have an assigned value that can be called upon during the running of the program, evaluated, and results output in different ways.

5.3 Blocks

We are going to create several scripts, and they will need to communicate in different ways. In some instances, we will use variables, but we will use messages mostly when programming with Scratch. Blocks of code are used on this platform to trigger scripts just the way the keyboard keys do when pressed. When a script is set to broadcast a message, all the scripts will be triggered to start with 'When I Receive…"

Just like variables, each message will have an assigned name when we create it. It must also be linked to a script which will trigger it to initiate a broadcast.

Now that you know variables and messages, we can begin designing our simple game.

5.4 Creating a simple arcade game based on the popular Ping pong

We are going to create a simple Ping pong game from scratch using Scratch and call it Punk Pong. Sounds catchy, doesn't it?

Ping Pong is an old arcade one or two player video game featuring a ball and two bats. The game is played by preventing the ball from touching the player's goal i.e. beyond the bat. It looks something like this:

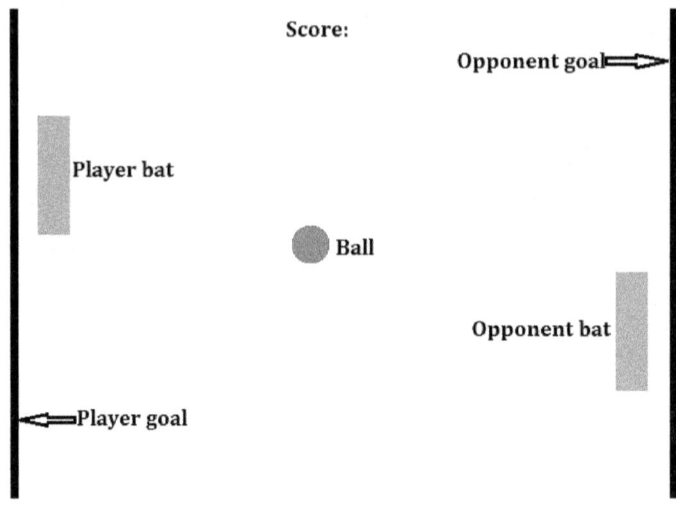

Fig 2: Layout of the Punk pong game we are going to create.

Step 1: Setting up Scratch

The first thing we will do is start a new workspace on scratch. When you open the program window, there will be the cat scratch by default. Right-click it and click 'Delete'.

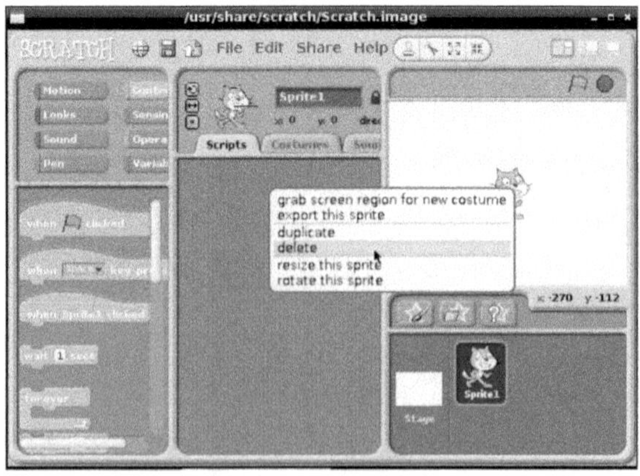

Fig 3: Creating a blank workspace

This will give us a free workspace to begin creating the game.

We are going to create five sprites for this game: The ball, player bat, opponent bat, player goal, and opponent goal.

Click on the 'Create New Sprite' icon and draw the ball. You will first need to select the color, then draw on the canvas and fill the ball with paint of the same color using the bucket tool. To draw a perfect circle and not an oval, press SHIFT on the keyboard while drawing.

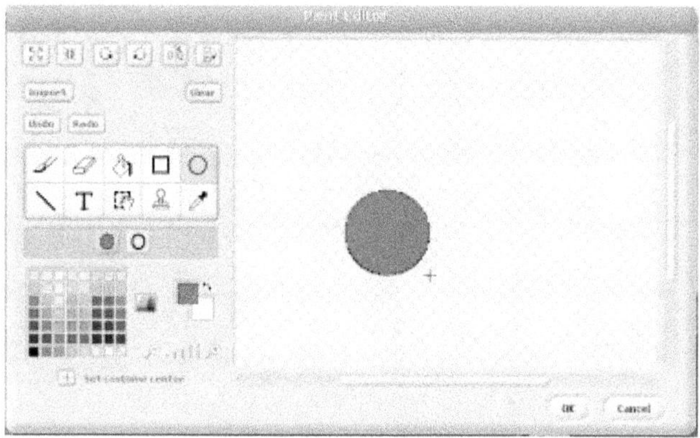

Fig 4: Drawing the ball sprite

When done drawing, click OK then assign the sprite a new name: ball.

Using the same procedure, create the remaining four sprites, making sure to assign them appropriate names:

- playerbat
- opponentbat
- playergoal
- opponentgoal

Once you have created and saved all the objects, you can drag them around the screen and place them in their rightful positions as in Fig 2.

Step 2: Making the ball bouncy

Double-click on the ball sprite. Its scripts section should be blank, but we can make it move around by adding a few instructions.

On the left section of the workspace, click on the orange 'Control' button to reveal associated steps under it.

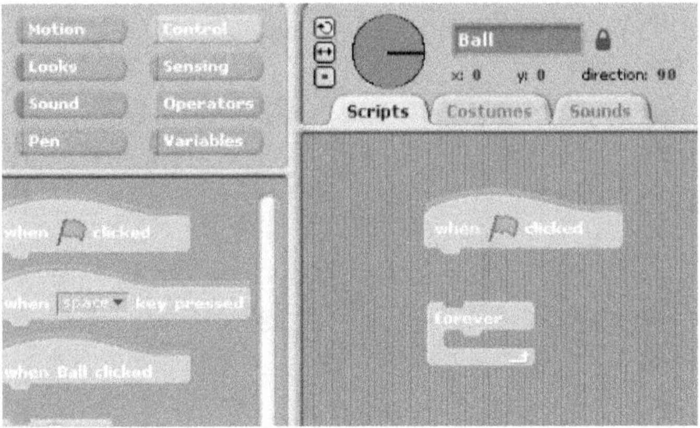

Fig 5: Programming the ball

Add the 'when clicked' piece with a green flag to the ball's logic then drag to position it high on the workspace.

Click on the '**Motion**' button and choose the 'point in direction' code then fit it under the first. Adjust the angle inside the block to 45.

The 'forever' orange loop block should fit after the 'point in direction' code. Click on the '**Motion**' button again and add 'move 10 steps' to fit inside the forever block. Change the steps from 10 to 5. This essentially means that the ball will move 5 steps in a 45 degree direction over and over again when clicked.

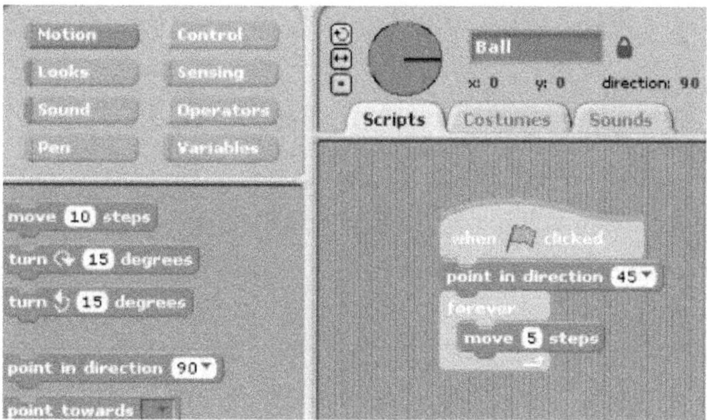

Fig 6: Programming the ball

To ensure that the ball is set to the center of the screen when the game starts, we will add a 'go to' piece defining the position as x and y coordinates. This will reset the ball position when the green start flag is clicked. We will also want the ball to bounce off the edges, we will add more code blocks as shown below:

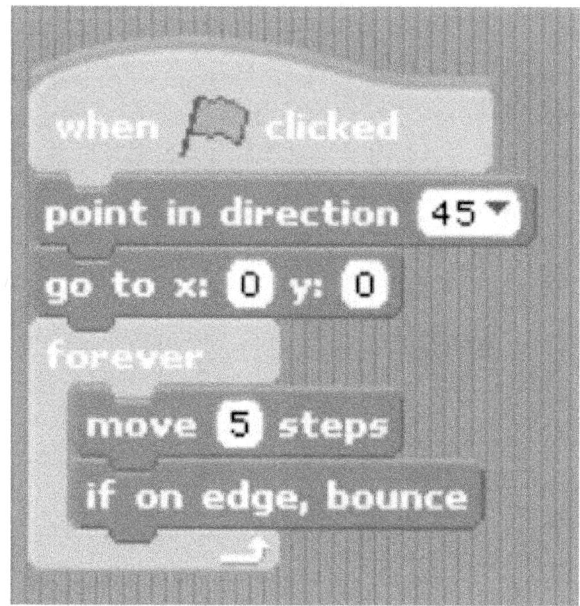

Fig 7: Defining the bat edge and centering the ball

Step 3: The ball and the bat

The players can defend their goals by getting the ball to hit the bat and bounce off it. We are going to program the ball such that when it hits a bat, it bounces off in a random direction.

Drag two orange 'if' blocks and position them after the last instruction within the 'forever' block. You can also alter the direction of the ball by clicking the rotate button to its left. The result should look like this.

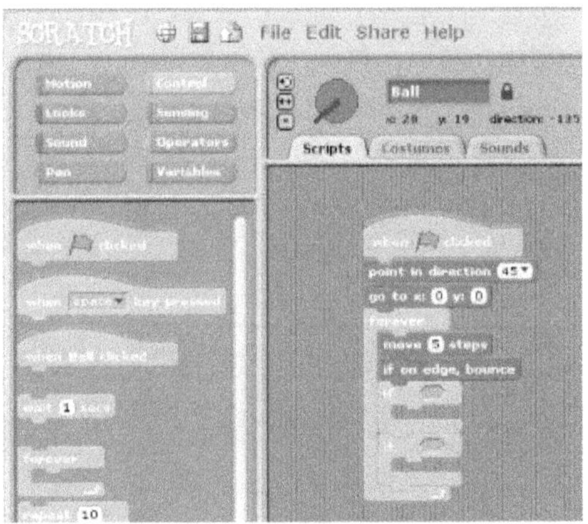

Fig 8: The ball and the bat

The two 'if' blocks will only execute the blocks within them when a condition they test equals true. We will insert conditions from the 'Sensing' button, dragging 'touching' to the 'if' blocks and changing the first to ***playerbat*** and the second to ***opponentbat***.

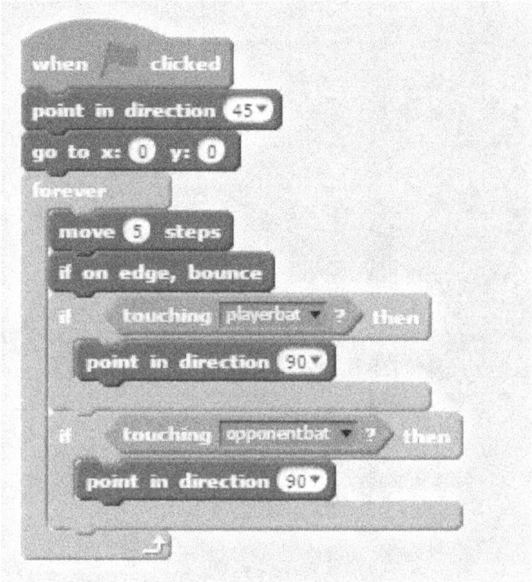

Fig 9: Programming ball bounce

We will also need to insert actions of code to execute when the conditions being tested return true. In this case, we will add point in direction blocks to each of the 'if' statements blocks and find an operator from the '**Operator**' button. We will then randomize the angle between 10 and 170.

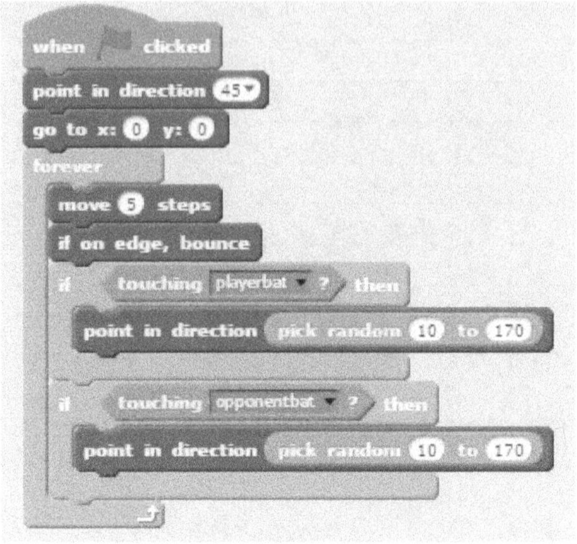

Fig 10: Randomizing the ball bounce

Fit the 'pick random' operator nicely within 'point in direction' block to randomize the direction the ball takes after hitting the playerbat or the opponentbat.

Step 4: Configuring player control

For the game to be playable, the player should be able to control the playerbat. We will program it such that the playerbat can be moved up and down the Y axis using the mouse.

Double click the playerbat sprite and add the objects as shown in the image. The process is pretty much the same as when you programmed the ball.

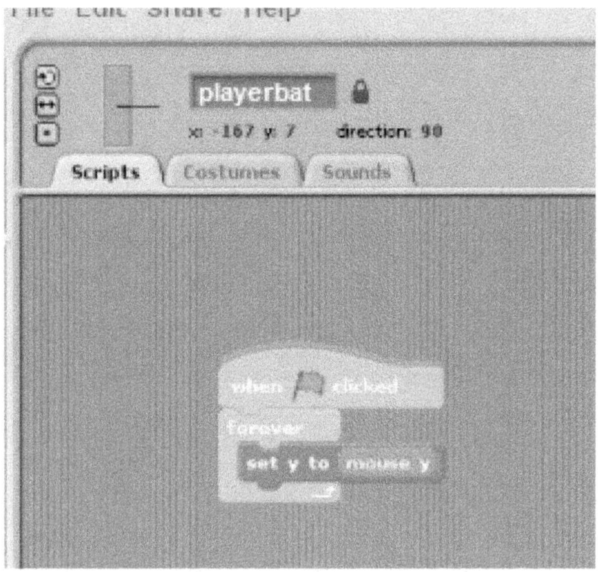

Fig 11: Setting up player input

When the player moves the mouse button up and down, the **playerbat** sprite will move along with it. Click on the green flag to test it out.

Step 5: Program the opponentbat to play intelligently

We are going to make our game playable by automating the opponent. Punk pong will be a single player game where the player plays against the computer. To make an intelligent opponent, we are going to dabble in some Artificial Intelligence.

Artificial intelligence is basically programming the computer to make decisions based on the information it receives. We will want the computer, in this case opponentbat, to prevent the ball from touching the opponent goal. This means that as the ball moves up and down the Y axis, the computer's bat should move along with it.

Double click on the **opponentbat** and blocks as shown in fig 12.

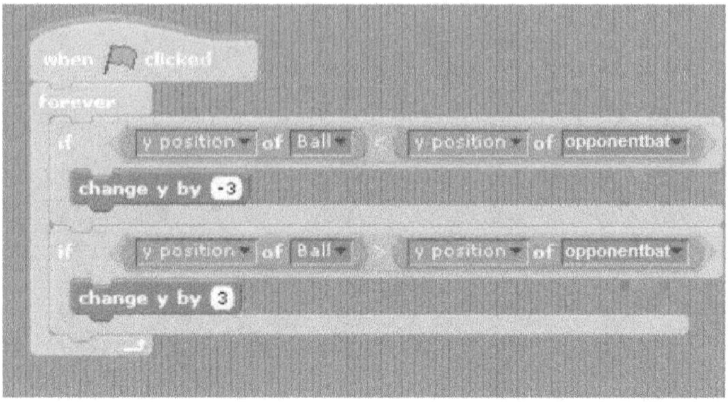

Fig 12: Programming computer opponent player

At this point, your Punk pong game is playable, but it cannot keep scores. We are going to make it even more interesting in the next step.

Step 6: Variables and keeping score

At this stage, we are going to create two new variables for scores: one for the player and another for the opponent.

Click on the red '**Variables**' menu item then click 'Make a variable'. Give it a name such as 'Player Score' then click on the 'For all sprites' radio button and click OK. Do the same for the 'Opponent Score'.

You should notice that a little counter is automatically added to the game screen.

Double click the ball sprite again to bring up its script code. To reset the scores at the beginning of the game, add two new code blocks just below 'when clicked' as shown:

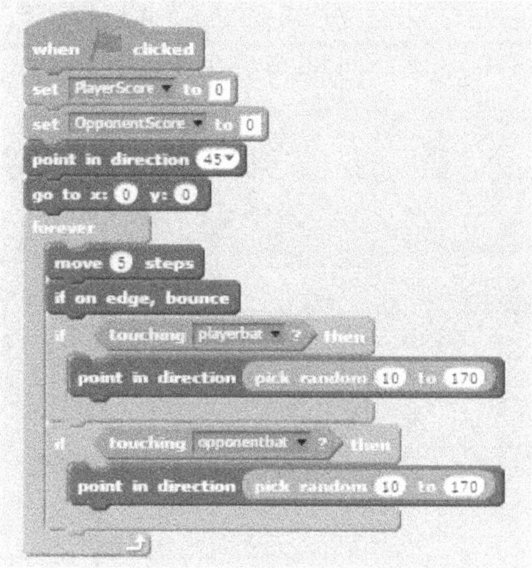

Fig 13: Randomizing ball bounce

The next thing we will do is configure the game such that when the ball hits the goal, the score increases by 1. We are going to add this code within the 'forever' loop. Modify your blocks to look like this:

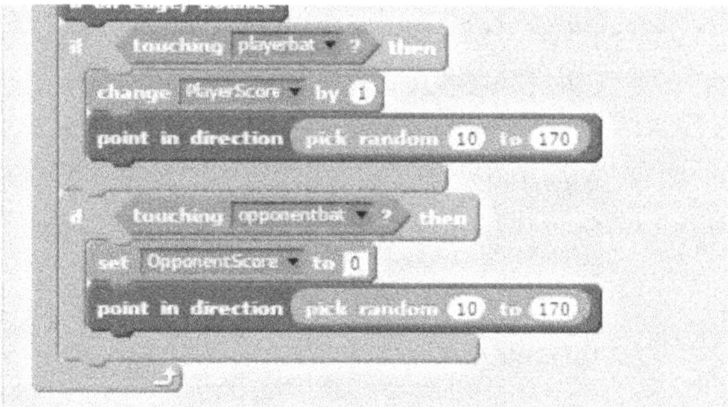

Fig 14: Configuring scores

Finally, we can add conditions to test to end the game if they return positive. In this case, we can set the game score to 5. When the ball touches the player's or opponent's goal five times, the game ends. Add two if conditions within the 'forever' loop and add a condition to test the scores for each as shown.

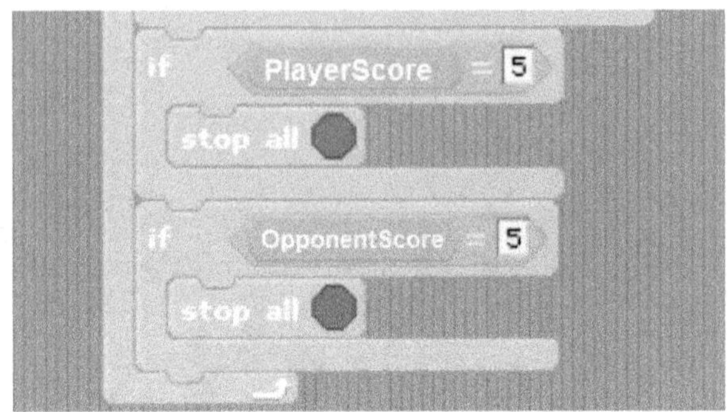

Fig 15: Programming game end

The 'stop all' block with a red stop sign ends the game.

5.5 Conclusion

Congratulations on completing your first game on Raspberry Pi. You can now test your game, and go back to the editing table to improve the drawings and even tweak other blocks in the script.

In the next hour, we will briefly look at what GPIO is and how it works, then we can figure out how to program Punk pong to output signals through it.

Hour 6: The GPIO (General Purpose Input and Output)

The GPIO pins of the Raspberry Pi are one of the most outstanding features of the board that makes it a favorite platform for budding programmers. These pins are the interface point through which the computer can communicate with other circuits and devices such as extensions boards and custom circuits. We are going to make some pretty cool stuff that make use of these pins.

Before we can get to that point, we first have to know the basics about them.

Warning: Experimenting with the GPIO pins can be very risky. A little short circuiting could brick your Pi, just like that. You should read widely about what to plug in to the pins and how to be careful not to cause damage to your board through proper insulation and care handling.

6.1 Understanding the GPIO on Raspberry Pi

Before you can begin working with the GPIO pins on your Pi, it is vital that you understand what the different types of pins there are, how you can enable the modules, and get to know what a breakout kit is.

Assuming that you own a Raspberry Pi 3, your board should have 40 pins in total, arranged in two rows of 20. Earlier models of the Pi had had 26 pins.

The pinout table below is a layout of the functions of the 40 pins:

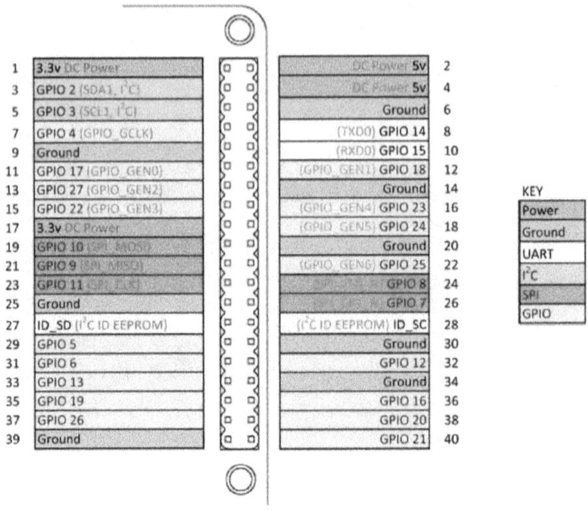

Fig 16: GPIO Pins (Image source: mcmelectronics.com)

As you can see on the color-coded image, there are more than just standard pins on the GPIO. Let us look at what each of the different types of pins refer to.

Power pins: These are pins that pull power directly from the Pi board. There are two types of pins—pin 1 and 17 that draw 3.3v and pin 2 and 4 that draw 5v.

GND: These are pins that are used to ground connected devices. It does not matter which ground pin you connect to, they are all the same.

UART: UART is an acronym for Universal Asynchronous Receiver and transmitter. The UART pins are serial in nature and are used to communicate with devices that support asynchronous interfaces.

I2C: This stands for Inter-Integrated Circuit, hence the square symbol after the I. It is acceptable to refer to it as I2C. These pins are used to connect hardware modules that support the I2C protocol. Typically, a device using this interface will be connected to two pins.

SPI: SPI is an acronym for Serial Peripheral Interface Bus. SPI pins are used to connect devices that support the SPI protocol to enable the Pi to 'talk' to them. It is pretty much similar to I2C except that they use different protocols to communicate.

GPIO: GPIO are the standard pins that are used for simple tasks such as turning devices on and off. We will be connecting our LEDS to these pins.

You do not need to memorize this table, or the definitions of the acronyms. What is important is that you understand what they actually do. With time and experience, you will get to master the purpose of each type of pins as the jargon and abbreviations will begin make more sense.

We recommend that you print out the pin layout chart provided along with this eBook as bonus material and stick it somewhere close to your work bench so that you can refer to it any time you need to.

In the next hour, we will take a step further into the world of programming the Raspberry Pi hardware by extending the capabilities of our Punk pong game.

Hour 7: Making an LED Blink with Scratch GPIO on Raspberry Pi

In the last six hours of learning how get around the hardware and software of your new Raspberry Pi, we have been covering the basics. What we will cover in this hour is also basic, but it is a stride in that it brings together two elements that are seemingly separate yet can seamlessly work together: writing a program that makes a hardware do things.

The whole point of learning to program with the Pi is to make the computer do solve problems by doing things. Otherwise we might just as well use your laptop to learn Linux and Python, or work with the online version of scratch accessible via your browser. You have reason to be very excited this hour because it is an introduction to what you have been looking forward to do with your newest micro-computer.

7.1 Getting everything ready

For the exercises in this hour, you are going to need:

1. Raspberry Pi 3
2. The working Punk pong game we created in Hour 5.
3. A breadboard.
4. 1 LED bulb.
5. 1K Ohm Resistor (Brown, Black, Red)

5. 2 male to female jumper wires.

Note: It is important that you have a clear working space when working on, especially because there is always danger in working with electrical current, no matter how small the voltage. Working in a cluttered environment is a recipe for disaster because even the tiniest strands of wire can cause catastrophic short circuits that could brick your Raspberry Pi or even cause fires.

As you learned in the previous hour in the introduction to the GPIO, the Pi outputs two different voltages that we will use to power the Pi: 3.3 and 5V. If you took a short while off between the last and this exercise, spare a few minutes to familiarize yourself with the location of the power and grounding pins because that is what we will be using in this exercise.

7.2 Usage and basic capabilities of GPIO server

The version of Scratch for the Raspberry Pi that was released in September 2015, which also comes with the Raspbian Jessie operating system you installed on your Pi, introduces a new GPIO server. This tool is used to drive LEDs, HATS, buzzers and other devices and components. This exercise will serve to introduce the basics of what you can do with the GPIO server but there is a lot more you will discover on your own.

Before you can use the GPIO pins on the Pi, you must first initialize the GPIO server. There are three ways you can do this:

1. From the Edit menu, choose 'Start GPIO server' to turn it on. If the server is already running, the item on the menu will change to 'Stop GPIO server'.
2. Using the gpioserveron broadcast on Scratch. You can then use gpioserveroff to turn it off.
3. Simply save your project with the GPIO server running and the status will be saved. When you initialize your project, the GPIO server will be automatically enabled.

In our case, we are going to use the broadcast method to initialize the inbuilt GPIO server, which we can then program in our Punk pong Scratch game to light up the LED.

Without any further setup, we will be able to access the basics of the GPIO capabilities by simply dragging the broadcast blocks under the orange Control button.

7.3 Connecting the hardware

Before we can write the code that makes the magic happen, we will first prepare the platform: assembling the circuitry.

This book assumes that you have basic knowledge of how to use a breadboard, how to connect wires, and more importantly, how electricity works and why we require male to female jumper cables. If you are not well versed with this part of working with the Pi, we recommend that you take some time to read various online resources to bring you up to speed before you attempt these connections.

Assemble the LED bulb and the resistor in series as shown in the figure below:

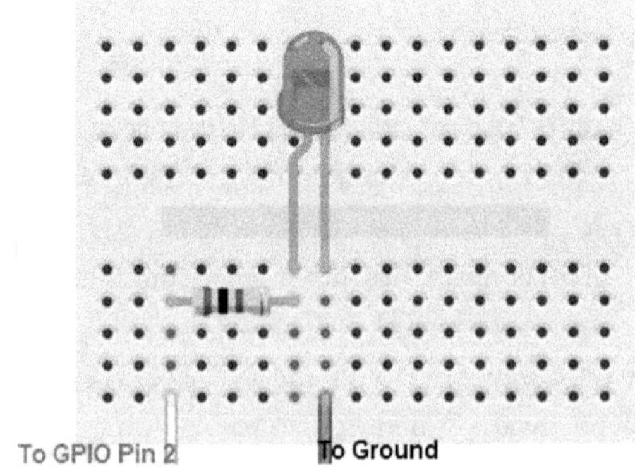

Fig 17: Connecting the circuits

Note that the longer leg of the LED is the positive, which you will connect to pin 2. The shorter leg is the negative, which connects to any ground pin on the Pi. Remember that ground pins are 6, 9, 14, 20, 25, 30, 34, and 39.

Use the female to male jumper wires to connect the breadboard to the GPIO pins on the Raspberry Pi.

When the connections are set, you can now move on to configuring our game to light up the LED.

7.4 Configuring GPIO pins on Scratch

Because we will be configuring the Raspberry Pi to send power to a pin of our choice when a certain condition is met, we must first define that condition. We can configure the game to trigger the LED light to turn on when an even occurs by finding its exact position on the script of the game.

For this exercise, we are going to configure the LED to light up when the player scores.

We are going to create three blocks for this: a broadcast block to turn on the pin when the player scores (we will be use pin 2), a block to delay the on status for the LED by one second, and another to turn it off.

Start your scratch app and load the Punk pong game we created. It should begin exactly where you left it.

We are going to add the two broadcast blocks to the script from the Control menu. Click on the orange Control button on the top left section of the screen then scroll down on the bottom section to find the broadcast block.

Considering that our game executes blocks according to the order they are arranged, we will then need to find the blocks that triggers the player's score.

If you remember well, it is the '*change PlayerScore by 1*' variable block within the forever block.

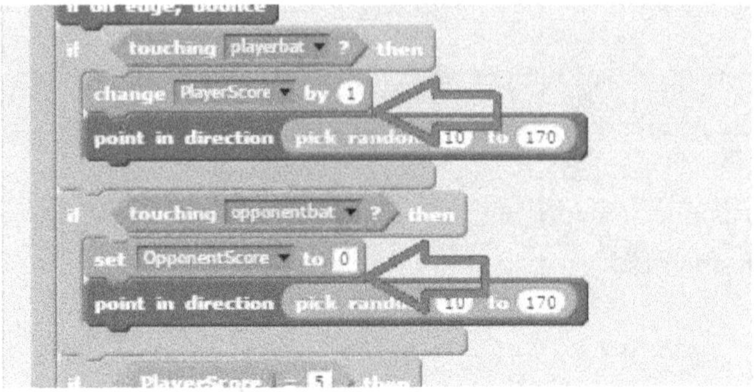

Fig 18: Where to program the GPIO broadcast

When you set a pin to be an output, it is connected to the Scratch sensor variable system. This means that it will appear in the list of possible values you can choose from the sensor blocks as well.

Drag the first broadcast blog and position it between the 'change PlayerScore by 1' variable block and the blue 'go to x: 0 y: 0' block. Next, designate the kind of signal you will send.

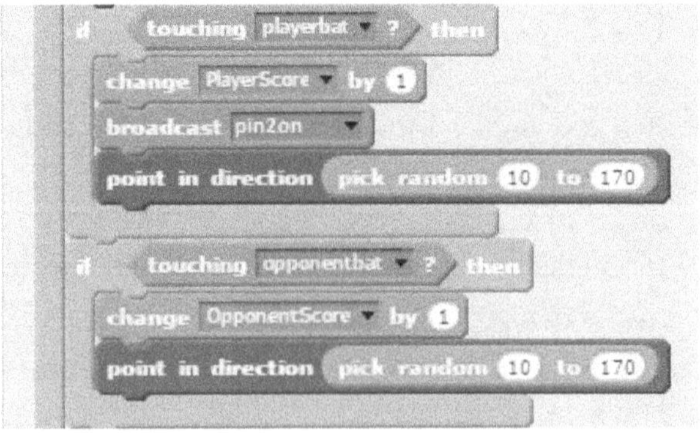

Click on the list box within the block to bring up a menu which allows you to enter a new command. Click '*new*' and when the input box appears, enter your new command.

Pins are defined by their numbers on the Raspberry Pi. What we will need to do is define the command in a similar format and the GPIO server will execute it without further configuration from our end. In this case, simply enter the message '*pin2on*' to turn on pin number 2.

Drag a '*wait 1 secs*' block and position it just below the one we just configured to turn on pin 2 on the GPIO.

We are going to leave its value the way it is but if you prefer you can change the duration of wait to 2 or 3 secs. You should not set it higher than that though because it will delay the reset and restart of the game for too long. Remember that Scratch executes the blocks in order, so if you set the wait for 10 secs, the LED will light for 10 seconds before the next block is executed.

Next, drag another broadcast block and position it beneath the '*wait 1 secs*' control block. Click on it to change its value, click new and on the input box, enter '*pin2off*'.

That is pretty much it.

In summation, the three blocks of scripts we added to our game will be triggered when the PlayerScore value increases by 1. The GPIO server will turn on pin 2 on, which will cause the raspberry Pi to supply 5v of power to pin number 2. This state will be maintained for 1 second (or whatever duration you specify on the '*wait 1 secs*' block and after that, power to the pin will be turned off and the game resumed.

You can also test the turn on and turn off broadcast commands by double-clicking the blocks. If they are properly configured, and the breadboard and GPIO pins properly connected, the LED should light right up.

Now, play the Punk pong game and see what happens when you score.

7.5 Conclusion

If your project was as successful as mine, you should be lighting up the LED every time you score in the game you created with Scratch. That was not difficult was it?

Scratch is an easy to understand and even easier to use programming platform that you can use for all kinds of content—not just games. There is also a lot you can make the Raspberry Pi GPIO server do besides light up a LED. Since you have already learnt the basics, you should go back to the beginning of hour 5 and create your own game, art, or storyline, and make it do all kinds of things using the GPIO server including checking the wiring operations of your circuitry.

Since we have done all this without any complex or detailed instructions, imagine what else you can do when you expand your learning environment and spend days, weeks, or even months working on it? The official Scratch website, https://scratch.mit.edu/, is resource-rich and has a vibrant community that has been creating and remixing all kinds of projects since 2012. Head on there to discover what else you can learn.

Hour 8: Introduction to the Shell on Raspberry Pi

When you installed Raspbian OS, one of the first things you discovered is that it has an easy to use graphical user interface similar to what you may be used to in Windows or Mac OS. Getting around the computer, creating and manipulating files, and managing packages is much easier with the interface. You can initialize your web browser by clicking on a link, start Scratch by double-clicking an icon on the desktop, and search for files by opening folder icons.

The thing is, a graphical user interface is not as powerful as a human-computer interaction point can be. This is where the command line interface (CLI) comes in. Because Raspbian OS is based on Linux kernel, its command line interface is known as the Shell or the Terminal.

8.1 What is the Shell or Terminal

The Shell, as we will refer the Raspbian terminal from this point on, is a text-based interface where you enter commands to get a response. If you are a Windows or Mac aficionado and have never encountered a command line interface before, do not worry. It may seem a bit confusing at first but with a bit of guidance and lots of practice, everything will begin to make sense and learning to use it will pay huge dividends in the near future, especially since you have shown interest in computer and machine programming.

To start the Shell on Raspbian, double-click on the LXTerminal program shortcut on the desktop or press Ctrl+Alt+T on your keyboard. The program window should look like Fig 21.

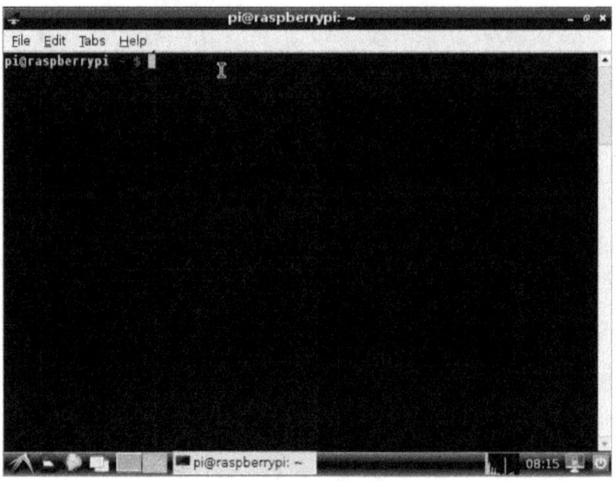

Fig 21: The LXTerminal running on Raspbian OS on the Raspberry Pi 3

8.2 Discovering basic commands in Unix

The line of text pi@raspberrypi ~ $ is the command prompt. This line shows that the system is ready and on stand-by to receive input from you. Enter the following and press enter:

pwd

What you entered is a command, in this case asking the Shell to Print Working Directory. This is simply a way to ask the Shell to show which folder you are currently working on. If you have not changed your username, it should return something like this:

pi@raspberrypi ~ $

/home/pi

pi@raspberrypi ~ $

The cryptic command pwd shows the default directory you start at when you initialize the shell. As you notice, after returning the first request, the shell will immediately take you back to the command prompt, ready for the next command. Now enter this new command:

ls

The horizontal list returned is a list of directories and files inside the present working directory. The ls command essentially shows the list of folders in the folder you are working on.

To move through the directories, you will use the cd command, which means change directory. Try it with this command:

cd Desktop

You should notice that your command prompt changes to:

pi@raspberrypi ~/Desktop $

This is the same as opening the Desktop folder on a graphical user interface. When you enter the **ls** command, it will show you the list of files and folders inside the Desktop folder. Try it.

To confirm that you are within the Desktop directory, use the command **ls**.

Now, enter the command:

cd –

The command **cd –** takes you back to the previous directory, in our case, the **/home/pi** directory.

When you want to go back to the home directory, no matter what your present working directory is, you can always use the command **cd pi** where pi is your username. You can substitute pi with your username if you have changed it on your Raspberry Pi. Another way to get to the home directory is by using the **cd ~** command wherever you are in the file system. The ~ symbol is pronounced tilde and always points to the home directory.

Now, while on the home directory, enter this command:

cd desktop

You should encounter an error:

bash: cd: desktop: no such file or directory

What is the problem yet our desktop spelling is correct, and we know a directory with such spelling exists?

It is the capitalization. In the shell, '**Desktop**' is not the same as '**desktop**', just the way '**cd**' is not the same as '**Cd**' or '**CD**'. When working on the shell, you must be very specific about the commands and file and folder names.

One of the best things about commands is that you can tell the computer exactly what you want and it will behave exactly as you want it to. You can expand on commands using flags such as the **–** (minus) we used after **cd** – to return to the previous directory.

With time, you will learn that there are so many flags to use with almost every command. For instance, to list all the files and folders in your present working directory including hidden ones, you will use the **ls** command with the **–a** flag. Your command will look like this:

ls –a

If you use the above command on the home directory, the number of files and folders on your list should increase.

Now try **ls –l**. What do you see?

How about when you combine **–a** and **–l** in the **ls** command to have **ls –al**?

8.3 Summary

There are hundreds of Linux commands you will learn while getting familiar with and mastering the Shell. This is the most basic introduction meant for absolute beginners. There are countless resources on the internet that provide lists of common and even most useful commands you can print out and stick to your refrigerator or on your workspace.

Now that you know how the command line interface works, you should do a bit of practice before you move on to the next of hour of study where you will be introduced to real programming: Programming the Raspberry Pi using Python.

Hour 9: Programming the Raspberry Pi with Python

If you are an absolute beginner to the world of programming, you must have been marveled at how easily you could write a playable game using the simple Scratch tool that comes bundled with Raspbian OS on the Raspberry Pi.

Scratch is a great tool for learning the basics of programming, and especially visualizing how a practical program works. However, sooner or later, you are going to run into its limitations and that is when you are going to need a more powerful and versatile general purpose programming language. At this point, I introduce you to: Python.

9.1 What is Python?

You have already heard the term Python (in programming, not the snake or the Monty python) but if you do not know what it is, it is a high-level interpreted and dynamic language that features readable code.

The design philosophy of this popular and general purpose language focuses on beautiful and readable syntax, which makes it easy for programmers to express their concepts for a computer in fewer lines of code.

Unlike scratch, which is also easy to learn, Python is entirely text-based. This does not mean that you cannot use Python to create graphics; it basically means that the program code is purely text and not drag-and-drop blocks.

The Raspbian OS you installed on your Pi comes pre-loaded with a python development environment (known as IDE for integrated development environment) which allows you to input commands and create your program syntax with a helper. The integrated environment comes with the handy help() command that will provide answers to questions you may need answers to as well as a built-in text editor which is color-coded to guide along, as well as automated placement of indents.

Because Python is text-based, you can use any text editor to write and save your code; you are not limited to using the IDE although it helps. There are many text editors you can download and use, some, such as *Leafpad*, come pre-installed with the Raspbian. *Geany* is a popular choice for new Python programmers and Sublime Text is my personal favorite. Python files are saved with the extension .py.

You should however not use word processors with advanced formatting capabilities such as LibreOffice and Microsoft Word. These programs introduce special characters to the code during formatting that will prevent your programs running correctly.

9.2 Hello World! on Raspberry Pi

It has become an accepted tradition for every programmer's first program to be a hello world program—a simple program that displays the worlds "Hello World!" on the screen. Because we assume this is your first programming that is exactly where we are going to start.

On the desktop of your Raspberry Pi, you should see a Python logo shortcut to Python 3 IDE named IDLE 3. It looks like this:

Fig22: Python 3 IDE Shortcut

Start the Python 3 IDE by double-clicking this shortcut or by going to the Pi Menu then Programming and Python 3.

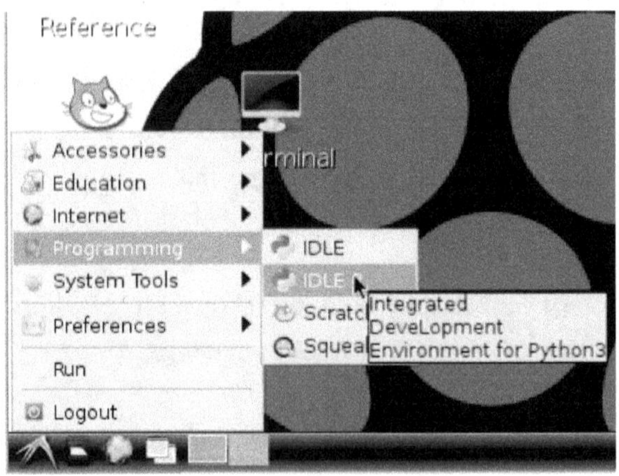

Fig 23: Starting the Python 3 IDE from the Pi Menu

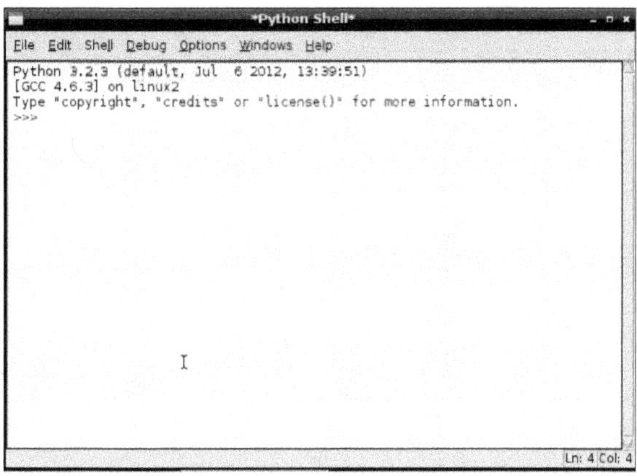

Fig 24: IDLE 3program window

Raspbian, and all Linux distros, ship with Python 2 interpreter by default. However, it is recommended that you always use the Python 3 interpreter because they two are significantly different.

When you are on the Python 3 IDLE window, enter the following code on the first line then press enter:

```
>>>print (“Hello World!”)
```

What this simple line of code does is tell the Python interpreter to print the phrase within the brackets and quotation marks on the computer screen. In this case, the phrase is Hello World.

Your line of code, however, is not saved in the computer memory, which is important when you want to create an actual program.

On the Python shell, click **File > New** to create a new blank text editor window to write and save your code.

On the new window, enter the hello world cord above. You will notice that the code is not run by the interpreter when you press enter. Save the code by clicking on **File > Save** or by pressing **Ctrl+S**. Give it the name **helloworld** and make sure that the file type selected is **Python Files** with extension **.py** or **pyw** before you click on the Save button.

9.3 Running a saved Python file

The best way for you to run a saved .py file is from the command line or the Terminal. Start the LXTerminal shell from the desktop. Ensure that your present working directory is the same one you saved the .py file. You can check using the command **pwd** and check the presence of the file using the command **dir**. In our case, the default directory is the same one we saved the helloworld.py file (/**home/pi**/).

Now enter the following command to run the file helloworld.py:

```
pi@respberrypi ~ $ python3 helloworld.py
```

An alternative approach is to first tell the system that the file you want to run is executable. You can do this using the command:

```
pi@respberrypi ~ $ chmod a+x helloworld.py
```

after declaring, you can then run the file using the command:

```
pi@respberrypi ~ $ ./helloworld.py
```

Note: Remember that names are case sensitive in the Terminal. Therefore, if you saved the file as "**helloworld.py**" and try to run "**Helloworld.py**", you will encounter an error.

If you run the program right, you should see the "Hello World!" text displayed on the screen. This shows that the program is running properly in the system, although at this point it is not a very useful program.

9.4 Learning to program Python

Python is a very simple to learn programming language but it is also very broad. We have created an in-depth 12 hour eBook that you can use to learn how to write programs that you can execute on your Raspberry Pi.

In this hour, we have covered what Python is and even created our first program to illustrate that you can create it on the Pi. However, we will not be covering the in-depth programming principles and how to create full-fledged programs in this book. We recommend that you check out our Python programming eBook 'Python: The No Nonsense Guide' if you are a beginner in programming for a complete guide.

9.5 Conclusion

The programs you will create for your Raspberry Pi using Python will be very practical in that you can use them to solve every day problems that you encounter. There are countless guides and ready-made tools and resources on the internet that you can use to simplify the process of designing and writing your own programs in Python. What is most important at this point is that you understand the process of creating and saving .py files and running them from the command line, all of which we have covered in this hour.

In the next hour, we will go in-depth to create a fully functioning Python app and run it on the Raspberry Pi. We suggest that you take some time between now and revert to Hour 10 and study as much as you can about programming in Python – the principles of correct syntax, importing libraries, and solving problems using simple code.

As a beginner in Python programming, and as a new owner of Raspberry Pi, it will not be long before you are a master in writing fully functional programs that make use of the hardware you have invested in. With a little practice and more studying, you will be able to program third-party hardware including sensors and output devices to make your Pi actually convert program code into action.

As a first step, we are going to dig deeper into Python on the Raspberry Pi and learn how we can make a LED light connected to a GPIO pin blink.

Hour 10: Writing More Code for Raspberry Pi in Python

We covered the introduction to Python in the previous hour and even went a step further to write out first program that writes text on the screen when run. You learnt how to run a .py file directly from the terminal using Python 3 and I mentioned that it was just the start. For this hour, we will cover more input and output of Python and write a simple code that can turn OFF and ON a LED light when certain conditions are met.

10.1 Input programming with Python

The input and output of a program are the most important for a budding programmer to learn, for the obvious reasons that the simplest functional programs must accept the user's input, process it, and give back a result.

While what we will create at this point may not be very useful, the most important thing you will learn is how to get the computer to do it. It is the principle and the method that matters. This will be starting point of the great things you will be able to program your Raspberry Pi to do – from building your own media center at home to developing an intelligent security system.

Start your Python IDLE from the desktop or by going to the **Pi Menu (Start) > Programming > IDLE 3**. We are going to write a simple program that will ask for the user's input then display the results.

First, we will learn about variables.

A variable is basically a reserved memory location that stores values. When you create a variable, you are asking the computer to reserve space in memory for a certain data type. The Python interpreter will allocate the memory such that the user input can be stored in.

We are going to create several variables for our new program. They are:

name = A string variable to store the user's name

yearofbirth = An integer variable to store the user's year of birth.

city = A string variable to store the name of the city the user lives.

profession = A string variable to store the name of the user's profession.

On your blank script, enter the following code exactly as it appears:

name = input ("Enter your name: ")

yearofbirth = input ("What year were you born?: ")

city = input ("In which city do you live?: ")

profession = input ("What is the name of your profession?: ")

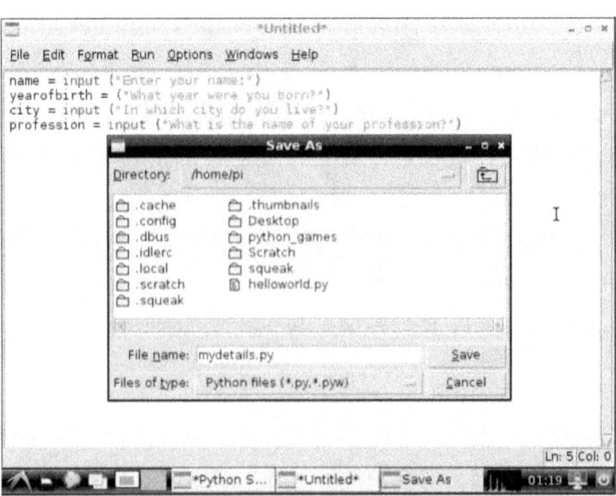

Save your code as *mydetails.py* or any other appropriate name you can think of, at a location you can easily access, preferably the default Pi directory on your Raspberry.

We are then going to run the code and see what it does. If you have forgotten how to run a .py file from the LXTerminal, go back to the last hour of this book to refresh your memory then try again.

If entered the code right, the program should prompt you to enter your name, the year you were born (in numbers), the city in which you live, and the name of your profession.

After you provide all this information, our program quits. This is because we have not programmed it to do anything further.

10.2 Adding comments to a Python script

There is no better point than this to introduce comments.

A comment in Python refers to something—text that is completely ignored by the Python interpreter. Comments are added to code as notes for yourself or other programmers who may want to understand what the code does. Comments are very important, as you will find out, and they are often preceded with the # (hash) symbol.

We are going to add comments to our code above to help us remember what the code does, and to tell someone looking at out code for the first time what it does. Modify your code to look like this:

```
#This program collects the user's details

name = input ("Enter your name: ")                    #Prompt for user name

yearofbirth = input ("What year were you born?: ")#Prompt for year of birth

city = input ("In which city do you live?: ")                    #Prompt for city

profession = input ("What is the name of your profession?: ")
        #Profession
```

When you save and run the above code, it will behave exactly as it did before you added comments.

10.3 Output programming in a Python script

Now that we have figured out how to make the Pi ask for information and the right way to leave comments on the code, we can go back to practicing making it output information.

We are going to add code that summarizes the name, age, city, and profession of the user. To achieve this, we will have to make a few modifications to the code like this:

```
#This program collects the user's details

name = input ("Enter your name: ")                    #Prompt for user name

yearofbirth = int(input ("What year were you born?: "))    #Prompt    for
year of birth and converts it to an integer.

city = input ("In which city do you live?: ")                #Prompt for city

profession = input ("What is the name of your profession?: ")
        #Profession

age = 2017 - yearofbirth  #Calculate age based on year of birth



print ("Hello. My name is", name, "and I am a", age, "year old", profession,
"from", city +".")
```

What does your program output when you run the code?

10.4 Programming the GPIO with simple code

Since you are already familiar with connecting an electrical circuit to use with the Raspberry Pi, this step will be much simpler. You are going to learn to program the GPIO pins by configuring the GPIO library and light up a LED bulb when a certain condition is met.

As with the experiment we carried out in hour 7, we are going to use the power pin number 2 on the Raspberry Pi board to supply the power to the LED and you will connect the cathode (negative) leg of the bulb to any ground pin.

Now, modify your code to look like this:

```
#This program collects the user's details

import RPi.GPIO as GPIO #Command to import GPIO library

GPIO.setmode(GPIO.BOARD) #Set the board to use pin numbering


name = input ("Enter your name: ")                    #Prompt for user name

yearofbirth = int(input ("What year were you born?: "))    #Prompt    for
year of birth and converts it to an integer.

city = input ("In which city do you live?: ")                    #Prompt for city

profession = input ("What is the name of your profession?: ")
        #Profession
```

age = 2017 - yearofbirth #Calculate age based on year of birth

print ("Hello. My name is", name, "and I am a", age, "year old", profession, "from", city +".")

GPIO.setup(2, GPIO.OUT) #Setup GPIO Pin 2 to OUT

GPIO.output(2,True) #Turn GPIO pin 2 to ON

When you run the above code, you will need Super User priviledges. Start the LXTerminal and use the command:

```
sudo python3 mydetails.py
```

If your LED is connected to the right pin and there are no errors in the code, the LED should light up when the code prints the output.

Should you encounter *ImportError no module named rpi.gpio*, chances are you did not run the code with super user privileges or you may need to configure your GPIO library. You can learn more about this on https://pypi.python.org/pypi/RPi.GPIO.

10.5 Making the LED light blink

Making an LED light up with a simple Python code is no easy fete; you are on your way to doing wonderful things with your Raspberry Pi board. As a bonus for this hour, here is a simple code that you can use on your current script to make the LED blink rather than just light up.

Go through the code and try to understand what each line does then implement modifications of your own to make the light do all kinds of crazy things. Remember to add comments of your own as proof that you understand what the code does.

Good luck.

```
import RPi.GPIO as GPIO #Import GPIO library
import time # Import the 'time' library to use 'sleep'

GPIO.setmode(GPIO.BOARD) #Use board pin numbering
GPIO.setup(2, GPIO.OUT) # Setup GPIO Pin 2 to OUT
#Define the Blink() function
def Blink(numTimes,speed):

    for i in range(0,numTimes):#Run loop numTimes

print "Iteration " + str(i+1)#Print current loop

GPIO.output(2,True)#Switch on pin 2

time.sleep(speed)#Wait time

GPIO.output(2,False)#Turn off pin 2

time.sleep(speed)#Wait


print "Complete" #When loop is complete, print "Complete"

GPIO.cleanup()

## Ask user for total number of blinks and length of each blink

iterations = int(input("Enter total number of times to blink: "))

speed = int(input("Enter length of each blink(seconds): "))

#Start Blink() function.

Blink (iterations), float(speed)
```

*Note: Indentations is very important. Observe it.

Hour 11: Reading and writing from GPIO ports from Python

Your decision to buy a Raspberry Pi was probably shaped by the knowledge that it is a board that has great extensibility—the capacity to connect many different external hardware to via the GPIO interface.

Even if you were not sure how much you could do with the Pi, by now, you probably already are planning a number of projects that could be classified as 'Physical Computing' because it involves programming third-party components and devices to be controlled by code written on the Pi.

In this 11th hour of the Raspberry Pi guide, we get to dive deeper into machine programming using the Python language and explore even further the powerful features of the Pi's GPIO pins majestically arranged on the top edge of your board. As you already know, these pins are the computer's interface to the outside world and at the simplest level, you can use them as input points you can connect sensors, and output points you can connect output devices.

11.1 Switching an LED on and off

In hour 10, we looked at how you can write Python code in a simple Python program we developed to turn on and off an LED bulb connected to the GPIO pins. We discovered that you need a Python library which provides a simple interface that you can use to manipulate everyday GPIO components. Luckily, because we installed the Raspbian OS, this library comes ready installed with the system.

But there is a simple way to manipulate an LED bulb without necessarily going around an existing code. This section of the book seeks to simplify how your Pi interfaces with both input and output hardware, and we will start with what we already know how to control – LED.

1. On your Raspberry Pi, start Python IDLE from the main menu. If you have forgotten, the process is Menu > Programming > Python3 (IDLE) or simply double click the shortcut icon on the desktop.
2. Start a new Python file and enter the following code:

```
import RPi.GPIO as GPIO

import time

GPIO.setmode(GPIO.BOARD)

GPIO.setup(2,GPIO.OUT)

GPIO.output(2,True)

Time.sleep(2)

GPIO.output(2,False)
```

3. Save your Python file and run it with administrator privileges (SUDO) to see what the code does.

An alternative approach to write a simple code that controls an LED bulb would look like this:

```
from gpiozero import LED

from time import sleep


led = LED(2)
```

```
while True:
    led.on()
    sleep(1)
    led.off()
    sleep(1)
```

With this Python code, you are choosing to use the BCM system of numbering the GPIO pins and not the BOARD system we used in the previous code. You can turn on the LED light using the code led.on() and turn it off using the code led.off(). For this example, the Python code will keep the LED bulb connected to Pin 2 flashing after every one second.

11.2 Connecting a push button to get input

As you can see from the example above, writing a simple code to control an output of electric current via a GPIO pin is pretty simple. But what would you need to do differently to program an input pin that controls a component, in our case a button?

For this demonstration, you are going to need:

1. Push button
2. Breadboard
3. female to male wire connectors.

Connecting a push button to your Raspberry Pi is as simple as connecting an LED bulb, except that we will use a different pin and a resistor is not necessary. In this case, we will use the listening port on Pin 3 (the second pin in the first row) and the other connection goes to any ground pin.

We will write a simple Python program that prints a short piece of text when the button is pressed.

Start your Python IDLE and create a new .py file with the following code:

```
from gpiozero import Button

button = Button(3)

button.wait_for_press()

print("Button Pressed!")
```

Save your code as a .py file, then connect the hardware as shown in the figure below:

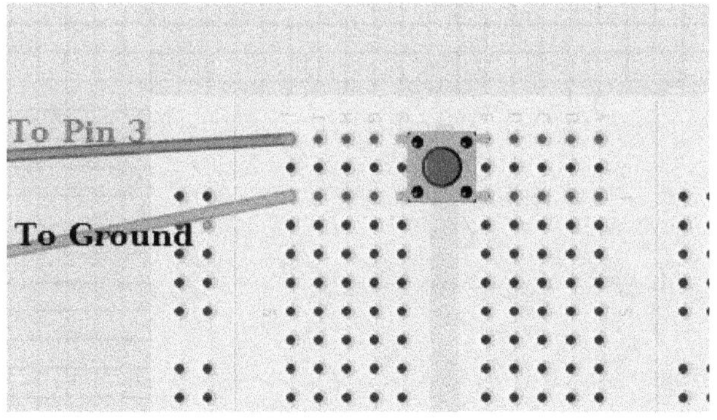

Fig :Connecting the push button to the Pins

Once your connection is in place, run the .py file from the Terminal with Superuser privileges. It should print text on the screen every time you push the button.

11.3 Controlling an LED bulb with a push button using Python

It will now be much easier for us to modify our program, and connect the LED bulb, such that when the button is pressed, the LED bulb lights up.

Modify your initial python program or open a new file from the IDLE platform and wnter the following code:

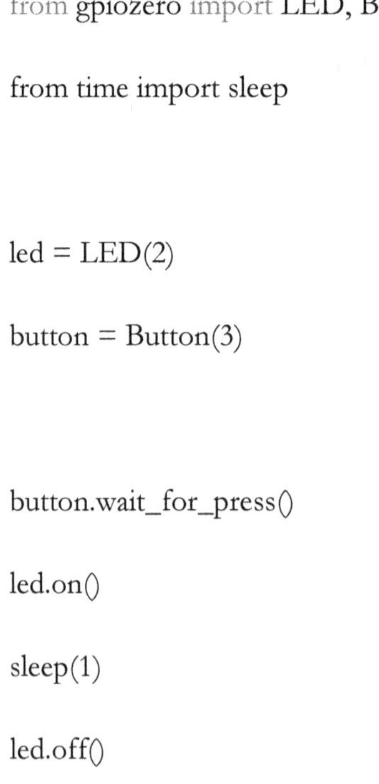

```
from gpiozero import LED, Button

from time import sleep



led = LED(2)

button = Button(3)



button.wait_for_press()

led.on()

sleep(1)

led.off()
```

If your connections are right, and you saved the code as it is, your LED bulb should light up for 1 second then turn off when you press the button on the breadboard.

Can you make modifications to the Python code to get three blinks of the LED bulb when the button is pressed?

11.4 Controlling the Brightness of an LED

So far, we have looked at how you can write a Python program that turns on and off an LED bulb. But how do you go about writing a code that can dim the light?

Raspberry Pi's RPI.GPIO library comes with a pulse-width modulation feature (popularly called PWM) that you can use to control the amount of power flowing from a pin to the LED, therefore controlling how bright it lights. In this example, you will connect the anode of the LED to pin 2 then run the code as a superuser.

```
import RPi.GPIO as GPIO

led = 2

GPIO.setmode(GPIO.BOARD)

GPIO.setup(led, GPIO.OUT)

pwm_led = GPIO.PWM(led, 500)

pwm_led.start(100)

while True:

    brightness = int (input ("Enter Brightness between 0 and 100:"))

    pwm_led.ChangeDutyCycle(brightness)
```

Tip: Whenever you connect an LED to your Pi, make sure that you connect a resistor in parallel between it and the board. The resistor serves to limit the amount of current that flows through the LED to a safe level, to protect both the LED bulb and the GPIO pin that is the source of power.

Warning: When playing about with the GPIO pins, it is important that you exercise caution to keep your experiments safe and fun. Connecting devices and plugging wires randomly to pins on the board and especially power sources is a very risky thing to do and could completely brick your board and even cause fires.

Bad things can also happen if you connect devices and components that require a lot of power. It is safer to do your initial experiments using 5V LEDS because they pose less risk. However, do not graduate to connecting motors before you have a firm grip on what you are doing.

If you are unsure about a device or a component, or just want to protect yourself and your devices, you can consider getting an add-on board—they are available online for a few dollars. You can use such a board until a time when you are confident enough to use the GPIO directly.

11.5 Programming a button that toggles an LED on or off

Suppose you want to add a power switch that turns the LED on and off when pressed? Considering that we have already figured out how to make a button work as an input and how to connect an LED to a 5V power source, this section will focus only on the code.

```
from gpiozero import LED, Button

from time import sleep


led = LED(2)

button = Button(3)
```

```
while True:

    button.wait_for_press()

    led.toggle()
```

This code toggles the state of the LED between on and off in a loop. If you want to make the LED switch only when the button is pressed and held down, you can use two methods of the button class: when_pressed and when_released. Your code would look like this:

```
from gpiozero import LED, Button

from signal import pause



led = LED(2)

button = Button(3)


button.when_pressed = led.on

button.when_released = led.off


pause()
```

Save your code in a .py file and run it from the command prompt with superuser privileges to test it out.

Hour 12: How to Get the Most out of your Raspberry Pi

The moment you connect and fire up your Raspberry Pi 3, if it is your first time doing so, the journey to a world of programmable computers that can do almost anything with simple code will have begun. And believe us when we say it will never stop.

Just a few years ago, it was almost impossible for hobbyist programmers and DIYers to attempt machine programming, especially at such a low cost. However, we can agree that tiny computers such as the Pi have opened up a world where anyone with a little passion and $50 can automate almost every aspect of their life.

In this guide, we installed the Raspbian OS to the Pi, a distribution of Linux that has the benefit of being easy to master and laden with all the tools a beginner would need. However, with time, you may need to try out the many other types of operating systems that you can use on the Raspberry Pi including those specially designed for security systems, for IOT connected devices, and even home media centers.

There is a lot you can do to get the most out of your Raspberry Pi. In this section, we will highlight some of the basic projects and steps you should consider as you graduate out of the beginner's circle.

12.1 Try different operating systems

At the beginning of this book, we briefly touched on a few operating system options available for you to install on the Raspberry Pi 3. The list was in no way exhaustive. While NOOBS has demystified how an operating system is installed on the Pi, and Raspbian has been put together to bring all the tools you need to get started, it would be wise for you to begin sampling what other operating systems available have on offer and what their benefits are. Some of the most popular operating systems you should consider trying are:

1. Android (RTAndroid): This is a regularly updated version of Android designed for the Raspberry Pi. If you are an Android developer, or just wish you could take advantage of all the free software available on Google Play Store to make your Pi a fully functional computer, you should check out the video tutorial about this OS here:
https://www.youtube.com/watch?v=cU7CEOmtmRk

2. Chromium OS: A group of passionate Rapberrians have come together to port Chromium OS to the Pi and other single board computers. So far, the group has released four editions of the ChromiumRPI. Note that this system is still in early developmental stages and should not be relied upon for everyday usage. You can check out what this OS is capable of on reddit here: https://www.reddit.com/r/chromiumRPI

3. Kali Linux: Are you a hacker or are looking for a dependable Linux distro for your security and penetration testing projects? If yes, then the ARM image of Kali Linux that runs smooth on the Pi may be what you are looking for. We have also written a complete eBook for beginners in hacking who may want to know how to get around Kali Linux tools called Hacking: The No Nonsense Guide. You can check out the eBook HERE. To see available images for your Raspberry Pi 3, go to
https://www.offensive-security.com/kali-linux-arm-images/

4. OSMC: The Open Source Media Center os for Raspberry Pi is exactly what you guessed it is – a feature-rich media center software for home projects. This OS is based on Kodi, formerly known as XBMC. It is very easy to set up and use and easily passes as one of the best media center systems available for the Pi. It is also a great system to set up for non-techy people who just want a functional system that does not require too much tweaking. You can read more about OSMC on https://osmc.tv/.

5. Windows 10 IoT Core: If you are a windows fanatic, the Windows 10 version for the Raspberry Pi is exactly what you hope it is. This is not the full version of Windows 10, it is just a development platform that you can use to prototype your IoT projects and test connected devices. Still, it is very functional although only useful if you have another computer running windows 10 around. Discover more about this OS on Github http://ms-iot.github.io/content/en-US/Downloads.htm

12.2 Get a case with a built-in heat sink

Some Raspberry Pi owners believe that a case for the board and a heat sink is not necessary. For normal use and experiments, you would not need to cool the chip unless its temperature exceeds 100 degrees Celsius. However, if you overclock the Pi or need to use it on demanding tasks that keeps the SoC on full speed performance for long periods of time, we suggest that you get a heat sink to prevent possible damage of your Pi.

You can order a case with inbuilt sink or order them separately. The casing may be particularly important if you want to protect the board from the elements like water and dust or static charge introduced by fabrics and such. If you are going to buy a case for the Pi, consider getting an official one from the Raspberry Foundation to support the guys that bring us this magnificent $35 computer.

12.3 Explore a world of amazing learner projects

This book covers a tiny fraction of the things you can do with the Raspberry Pi. A simple search on the internet would show you the amazing myriad of projects that beginners such as yourself have managed to create over the years. The best way to get inspired to create something new is to check out what other Pi users have done with their boards, and often with a few third party components and circuits.

With a little investment and effort, you can easily add a camera module to your Pi, connect a touchscreen display, set up your own server, or even create your own cloud storage. In fact, if you are feeling ballsy, you can even buy a few sensors online and install a Raspberry Pi to autonomously drive your car!

The best part of this all is that you will be able to get support from the millions of users who share their code, tips, and tricks online on Reddit, social media, Stack Exchange, Github, and blogs. You can find some of the top places to seek inspiration in the section below.

BONUS #1: Raspberry Pi 3 Pinout Chart

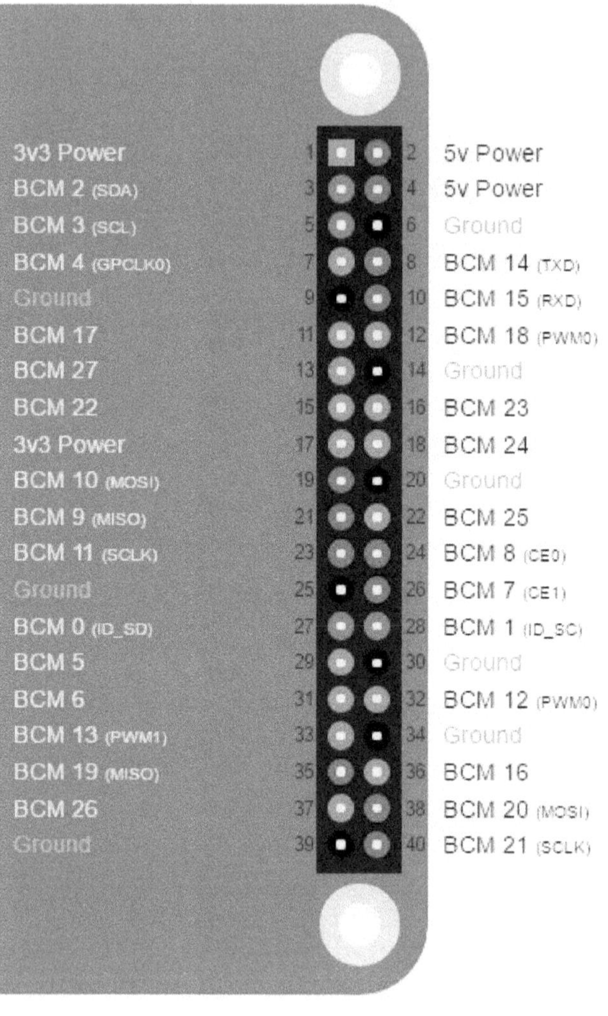
3v3 Power
1
2
5v Power
BCM 2 (SDA)
3
4
5v Power
BCM 3 (SCL)
5
6
Ground
BCM 4 (GPCLK0)
7
8
BCM 14 (TXD)
Ground
9
10
BCM 15 (RXD)
BCM 17
11
12
BCM 18 (PWM0)
BCM 27
13
14
Ground
BCM 22
15
16
BCM 23
3v3 Power
17
18
BCM 24
BCM 10 (MOSI)
19
20
Ground
BCM 9 (MISO)
21
22
BCM 25
BCM 11 (SCLK)
23
24
BCM 8 (CE0)
Ground
25
26
BCM 7 (CE1)
BCM 0 (ID_SD)
27
28
BCM 1 (ID_SC)
BCM 5
29
30
Ground
BCM 6
31
32
BCM 12 (PWM0)
BCM 13 (PWM1)
33
34
Ground
BCM 19 (MISO)
35
36
BCM 16
BCM 26
37
38
BCM 20 (MOSI)
Ground
39
40
BCM 21 (SCLK)

BONUS #2: The Top 6 Raspberry Pi Projects for Beginners

We all agree that Raspberry Pi, despite being credit-card sized, is a very dynamic microcontroller that has the capability to do just about anything you program it to do. It runs on the powerful Linux kernel and you can program it with plain Python language. There is no greater way to learn about coding and hardware hacking than through Raspberry Pi projects.

This is why we have put together a list of 6 of some of the best projects beginners like yourself have shared with the world. They should be inspiration enough to make you want to try them and even conceive better project ideas that you will share with the world.

1. DIY Raspberry Pi Music Player

In this project, you build your own music center using prebuilt software such as Pi's Musicbox and use a different device to control it such as your phone or remote controller.

Requirements

- Raspberry Pi
- 8 GB microSD Card
- Ethernet Cord or Wifi router
- Internet connection
- Mouse
- Keyboard
- USB drive

Link: https://pimylifeup.com/raspberry-pi-music-player/

Credit: Gus

2. Raspberry Pi Twitterbot

Wouldn't you like to make a bot that lives in your Raspberry Pi and interacts with the world via twitter? A builder on Instructables has done just this, in a project called Bot Collective to make Twitter bots that have physical Pi bodies and use the Twitter engine to communicate. You too can build one using the instructions made available.

Requirements:

- Raspberry Pi
- Mouse
- Keyboard

- Internet connection
- Second computer
- Smartphone

Link: http://www.instructables.com/id/Raspberry-Pi-Twitterbot/?ALLSTEPS

Credit: scottkildall

3. Raspberry Pi Personal Assistant.

Build a voice-controlled device using parts from an intercom system and a sound card. The guide on instructables will show you how to connect to the Pi via the intercom, install voice controller software, and add speech scripts that will return as audio outputs.

Requirements

- Raspberry pi.
- USB WiFi adapter
- USB soundcard
- Small 5V amplifier
- A 5V DPDT (Double Pole Double Throw) relays
- Some wires

- USB keyboad and mouse
- TV with HDMI or video in connection for installing everything on the Pi

Link: http://www.instructables.com/id/Raspberri-Personal-Assistant/

Credit: janw

4. Raspberry Pi Weather Station

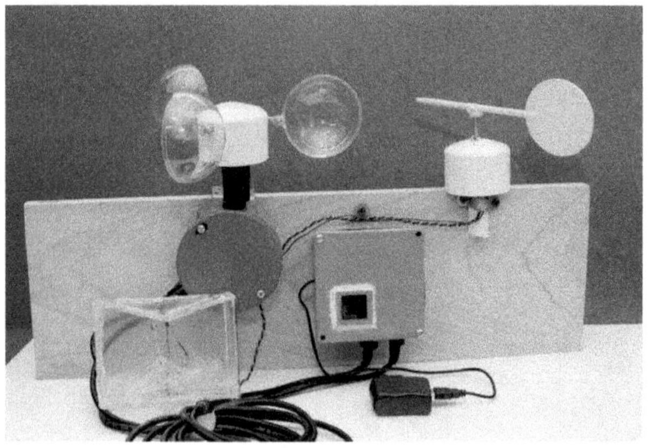

Well, you could always check the five day weather forecast on TV or add a widget to the homescreen on your phone, but where is the fun in that when you can build a weather station of your own? This Raspberry Pi project does just that. You can accurately read temperature, wind speed, humidity, and atmospheric pressure among others with a simple build.

Requirements

- Raspberry Pi
- Pi camera
- Reed switches
- Sensors
- USB GPS chip

- Magnets
- MCP3008 chip
- Resistors
- Wireless adapter
- Waterproof case

Link: http://www.instructables.com/id/Complete-DIY-Raspberry-Pi-Weather-Station-with-Sof/?ALLSTEPS

Credit: kkingsbury

5. Raspberry Pi Wall Mounted Google Calendar

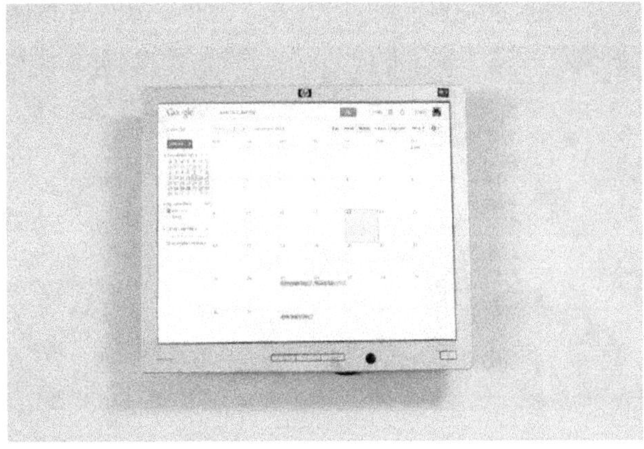

The ultimate step of setting up a home personal assistant is how it communicates with you. One of the best implementations of a house assistant is by making a wall-mounted communication point, in this case, a digital calendar run by Raspberry Pi. This instructable will help guide you to understand general home networking and computing and how to bring the power of google into your tiny home computer.

Requirements

- Raspberry Pi

- Working home connection (Ethernet or Wi-Fi)
- Memory card
- AC Adapter
- USB wireless mouse and keyboard
- Wall mountable monitor with HDMI
- Wall bracket

Link: http://www.instructables.com/id/Raspberry-Pi-Wall-Mounted-Google-Calendar/

Credit: Piney

6. Raspberry Pi Personal Cloud Storage

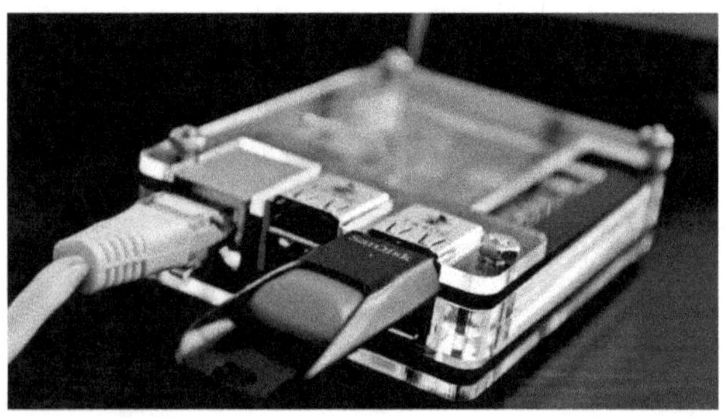

In this project, you can learn how to make your own cloud storage using Raspberry Pi. This is a computing system that will store your data on a local network to save you the bandwidth cost of constantly uploading and downloading data for local use. You will also be able to access your files from any connected computer over the internet.

Requirements

- Raspberry Pi
- Memory card

- Internet connection (Ethernet or Wi-Fi)
- External hard drive or USB drive
- USB keyboard and mouse
- Powered USB hub

Link: https://pimylifeup.com/raspberry-pi-owncloud/

Credit: Gus

So, which one of these projects are you going to start with?

www.ingramcontent.com/pod-product-compliance
Lightning Source LLC
LaVergne TN
LVHW022309060326
832902LV00020B/3365

* 9 7 8 1 5 4 4 2 7 1 9 7 2 *